EMPIRE
FLYING BOAT

1936 to 1947 (all models)

COVER CUTAWAY: Short S.23 'C' Class Empire flying boat. *(Mike Badrocke)*

First published in 2013

A catalogue record for this book is available from the British Library.

ISBN 978 085733 0796

Brian Cassidy has asserted his moral right to be identified as the author of this work.

Library of Congress control no. 2012936194

Published by Haynes Publishing,
Sparkford, Yeovil,
Somerset BA22 7JJ, UK.
Tel: 01963 442030 Fax: 01963 440001
Int. tel: +44 1963 442030
Int. fax: +44 1963 440001
E-mail: sales@haynes.co.uk
Website: www.haynes.co.uk

Haynes North America Inc.,
861 Lawrence Drive, Newbury Park,
California 91320, USA.

Printed in the USA by Odcombe Press LP, 1299 Bridgestone Parkway, La Vergne, TN 37086.

Acknowledgements

I would like to thank the many people who have helped me over the years with material for this book, some of whom worked on the Empire 'boats in No 3 Shop at Rochester and knew them in detail, inside and out.

It has been a privilege to meet other 'old hands', Imperial Airways Captains amongst them, who had kept fresh a vivid recollection of their time on the 'boats – what it was like to maintain them, fly them on the routes, look after the passengers and to be one of the few who experienced a journey by peacetime in an Empire flying boat.

The Second World War brought a much more violent second chapter to the history and a new dimension to flying boat operations worldwide. The 'boats cut off at the eastern end of the Horseshoe Route to Australia and New Zealand were often in the thick of it.

The history of Short's Empire flying boats stretches back nearly 80 years, but luckily some photographs of the 'boats remain. In the intervening years many have passed through so many hands and are now so widely dispersed on the Internet that it is often impossible to attribute sources. All reasonable efforts have been made to determine copyright ownership, but I would like to apologise if anyone's copyright has been inadvertently infringed.

My grateful thanks go to Paul McMaster of Short Brothers plc for supplying photographs and for permission to reproduce these photographs and diagrams. The detailed photographs of the 'boats under construction were taken in the Erecting Shops at the Seaplane Works in Rochester by Mr V.E. Galloway, with his plate camera.

I am grateful to the British Airways Speedbird Heritage Centre and to Paul Jarvis and Jim Davies in particular for their valued help in supplying many of the photographs and illustrations that grace these pages.

Thanks, also, to Mike Badrocke for permission to reproduce his excellent cutaway drawing of the Empire 'boat used on the cover and inside the book.

My photocopy of Major Mayo's Empire Maintenance Manual was supplied by the Science Museum in London. I have it bound in original covers given to me by Eddy Gosling, one of the Shorts draughtsmen who drew the original diagrams. The RAF Museum at Hendon supplied my copy of the Short S.23 Type Record.

Being of the generation which still draws with a pencil on film on a drawing machine, I would like to thank Len Whalley who digitised my general arrangement drawing of the S.23 and whose sharp eye on the text was of great help. My thanks also go to Peter Hunt for his assistance with preparation of the text.

Lastly, I would like to thank Jonathan Falconer at Haynes Publishing, who kept me on the straight and narrow with help and encouragement.
Brian Cassidy,
Bath, September 2012.

EMPIRE FLYING BOAT

1936 to 1947 (all models)

Owners' Workshop Manual

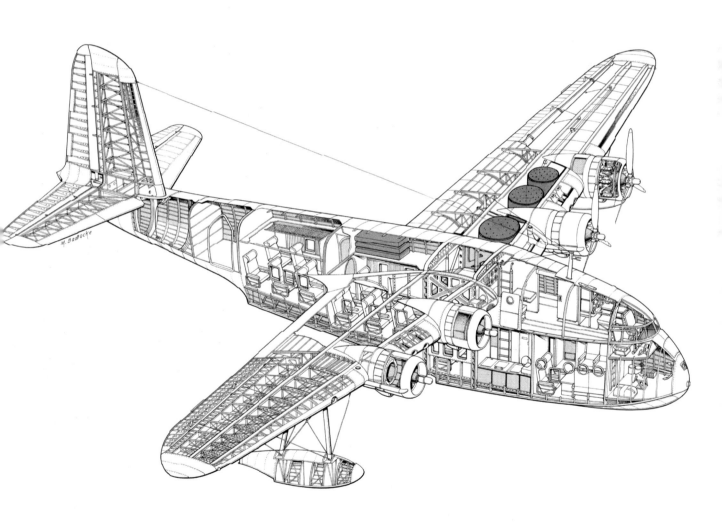

An insight into owning, servicing and flying the
Short 'C' class Empire flying boat

Brian Cassidy

28
HYDRAVIONS TYPE 'EMPIRE'
VITESSE : 320 KILOMETRES HEURE

IMPERIAL AIRWAYS

EUROPE   AFRIQUE   INDES
EXTREME-ORIENT   AUSTRALIE

Contents

OPPOSITE An Imperial Airways poster from the late 1930s depicting Empire flying boat *Canopus* in dock ready to board passengers. *(British Airways Speedbird Heritage Centre)*

Introduction

It may even be too late now to record the full story of the 42 – nearly 43 – Empire flying boats. Time and history move on quickly. Although some small scraps of the flying boats exist, none of the aircraft themselves have survived. So much about them has already vanished. Most of those who flew and worked the 'boats are, sadly, no longer here. For all practical purposes, the Short Brothers' drawings and most of the calculations have gone up in smoke and unless someone, somewhere, has a hitherto undiscovered hoard of prints, they too seem to have all disappeared.

The Empire 'boats had a highly respectable pedigree. They were designed and built by the world's first aircraft manufacturing company, led by one of the pioneers of metal construction for aircraft, Oswald Short, now seemingly forgotten. Oswald Short and Francis Webber designed the world's first metal-hulled flying boat, the minute Cockle. Arthur Gouge, with an apparently faultless eye for a flying boat hull, succeeded Webber as Chief Designer, to design the Singapore I and set the line of ancestry that led to the Empire hull. The Seaplane Works at Rochester built 27 flying boats of 8 different designs from the launch of the Singapore I in August 1926, to the roll-out of the first Empire 'boat ten years later.

The Empire 'boats were designed to carry the mail and for the first chapter of their history

they did so. The sections of this book outlining the operations of the 'boats on the Empire Air Mail Programme, and later on the Horseshoe Route and their wartime exploits, do no more than scrape the surface. A fully expanded account is needed to complete this corner of aviation history.

The fact that an authentic general arrangement drawing of an Empire 'boat could not be found is a considerable drawback. None of the existing three-view drawings, and most of them are no more than small-scale diagrams, are wholly accurate. Over the years, I have assembled – the correct word as the sources are many – a set of General Arrangement drawings. Until a print of an authentic Short Bros GA can be found to check these drawings, they are probably the best available. The drawing number for the hull lines is Short Brothers S.23.C.1000.

I was ten years old when *Canopus*, the first of the 'C' class, was launched, but to my certain knowledge I have never seen an Empire 'boat. Without the help of those I have met, who knew the Empire 'boats inside and out, there would have been little to add to their story.

Many of the photographs in this book have been provided by Short Brothers plc as prints of Mr Galloway's magnificent photographs. The S.23 'C' class Maintenance Manual in my possession is a photocopy of Major Mayo's, now lodged as part of the Mayo papers at the Science Museum. The photocopied text of this manual has been reunited with an original screw-bound hard cover, a gift of Eddy Gosling acquired during his time in the Drawing Office at Rochester. Permission to publish the photographs and the diagrams from the Maintenance Manual has been granted by Short Brothers plc and is acknowledged with thanks.

Brian Cassidy,
Bath, October 2012.

BELOW **Empire 'boats: Imperial Airways' G-AETZ,** *Circe,* **and VH-ABB,** *Coolangatta,* **of the Australian operator QANTAS.** *(British Airways Speedbird Heritage Centre)*

Chapter One

The 'C' class Empire story

The graceful form of the Short S.23 'C' class Empire flying boat can trace its ancestry to the company's Singapore 'boats of the twenties. With a faultless eye for a flying boat hull, Arthur Gouge, Shorts' General Manager and Chief Designer, conceived the Empire 'boat, the launch of which from the famous slipway at Rochester caused a sensation in July 1936.

OPPOSITE G-ADHL, *Canopus*, **wearing the Speedbird livery of BOAC, about to alight.** *(Author's collection)*

ABOVE When the Handley Page HP42 entered service with Imperial Airways in 1931, the biplane airliner opened a new chapter in air travel. This is HP42E, G-AAUD, *Hanno*, an example of the longer-range 'E' model ('E' for Eastern), usually known as the 'Hannibal' class to distinguish it from the standard European (or 'W' model) 'Heracles' class. Hannibals operated from Cairo on both the Indian and African routes.
(US Library of Congress)

BELOW Short S8 Calcutta flying boat, G-AASJ, *City of Khartoum*, was one of five operated by IAL. Pictured on the River Nile in 1932, 'SJ prepares to take off from Gaza to Cairo via Ismailia. (Three years later she crash-landed off Alexandria harbour.) *(US Library of Congress)*

Change in the air

By the middle of 1936, British commercial aircraft were fast becoming something of a joke. Imperial Airways Limited (IAL) was Britain's major airline and although its aircraft were considered comfortable and safe, most of them were biplanes and they were slow. IAL's No 1 European Operating Division had two Handley Page HP42s, two Short L.17 landplane versions of the Kent flying boat, and seven de Havilland DH86As – all biplanes. No 2 Division had five

Handley Page HP42s, three de Havilland DH86As and four flying boats, two Short Calcuttas and two Short Kents – all biplanes. Nos 3 and 4 Operating Divisions had eight Armstrong Whitworth AW.XV Atalanta monoplanes between them and one de Havilland DH86A. The fleet was completed with three other monoplanes, two Avro 652s and a single Westland Wessex.

Although cruising speeds are often quoted on the optimistic side, they are one rough-and-ready way of comparing performance and speed and that, for commercial operation, is important. The fastest passenger-carrying aircraft in the IAL fleet was the de Havilland DH86A, with a cruising speed of 126kts. The Atalantas cruised at 103kts and the Short Kent flying boats and the two L.17s, both at 91kts. The Handley Page HP42s cruised at 83kts and the Short Calcutta flying boats at 70kts.

In the United States, the Boeing 247 – the world's first 'modern' airliner – had been flying for three years with a cruising speed of 135kts. The Douglas DC-2 and the Lockheed L-10 Electra had cruising speeds of 172kts – approaching twice that of the L.17s – and had been flying for two years. The incomparable Douglas DC-3 entered service with American Airlines on 25 June 1936 – with a cruising speed of 180kts – just over a week before the flight of the first Short Empire flying boat at Rochester. These three American airliners changed the shape of airline economics,

bringing about the chance of profit by carrying passengers with some airmail supplement. Of the flying boats, the Sikorsky S.42 and the Martin 130 had cruising speeds of 148 and 136kts and both had been flying for two years.

But changes were about to take place in the British aeronautical world. The advent of the Empire flying boats caused a sensation. Written in March 1936, some four months before the launch of the first 'boat, an article in *Flight* stated: 'Never in the history of flying has there been a parallel to the activity in civil flying boat construction, the beginnings of which are now to be seen at the Rochester works of Short Brothers.'

But before we embark on the story of the Empire 'boats, first it is necessary to retrace our steps in time to the earliest days of powered flight before the First World War and the birth of the Short Brothers partnership.

Short Brothers – seaplane builders

Created in November 1908 to build gliders and aeroplanes, the Short Brothers partnership was formed by the brothers Horace, Eustace and Oswald Short. The Short family background had strong connections with mining and engineering in the industrial north of England. Samuel Short, the brothers' father, had been apprenticed to the great Victorian engineer Robert Stephenson and had managed

a coal mine at Little Chilton near Durham before moving on to become the chief engineer of the iron foundry at Stanton-by-Dale in Derbyshire. Horace, his eldest son, had worked at the Parsons steam turbine factory before leaving to form the partnership with his brothers.

Eustace and Oswald had previously established a balloon factory, first at Hove and then in the railway arches at Battersea in London, but having realised that aeroplanes were the future the partnership moved to Eastchurch on the Isle of Sheppey in Kent where they started the production of aircraft. Horace was already building gliders, and Eustace managed to get a flight with Wilbur Wright during his European tour. As there were no established drawings for the Wright aircraft, Horace produced a set of working drawings from the detailed measurements he had previously made of the aircraft. With these drawings, Short Bros obtained manufacturing rights from the Wright brothers for the construction of six Wright Flyers – the first aircraft-manufacturing contract in the world. In 1910 the Royal Aero Club offered to train four naval officers to fly. Part of their training was six months' technical instruction from Horace. The second trainee, Lt Arthur Longmore RN (later Air Chief Marshal Sir Arthur Longmore, GCB, DSO), began experimenting with Oswald on the use of aircraft at sea, leading to increased interest in the design and construction of the seaplane.

In 1913 the development of a larger site with waterside access was begun on the banks of the River Medway to the west of the city of Rochester in Kent. This was to be called the

LEFT An aerial view of the Shorts Seaplane Works taken from the west. From top left to bottom right along the river bank are Nos 1, 2, 3 and 4 Shops. No 3 Erecting Shop is the largest of the four. The end of the chalk dump is seen on the far right, behind No 4 Shop. The tide is out showing the slipway spanning the Medway mud to the water's edge. The Medway Tower, soon to be demolished, is still in place between Nos 3 and 4 Shops. The famous slipway was one of the first reinforced concrete structures in the country and designed to take loads of 20 tons, which meant that later it could be used for the Empires. (Author's collection)

Seaplane Works, a name it kept for the whole of its occupancy by Short Bros. In early 1915, No 1 Erecting Shop had been completed and the steel framework for No 2 Erecting Shop was up. By 1918, the new No 3 Erecting Shop was complete – a nine-bay structure, three bays wide by three deep, two bays of 100ft wide flanking a centre bay of 120ft. The production floor space of the new building more than doubled the total floor area of the other two Shops. A reinforced concrete slipway was built on the centre line of the main door of No 3 Shop, spanning the Medway mud to a point below the low-water mark so that aircraft could be launched at any state of the tide. It was designed to carry loads of up to 20 tons, which showed considerable foresight, as the most likely load at that time was 5 tons.

The entire workforce of about 300, one of whom was 23-year-old Arthur Gouge (later Sir Arthur and Chief Designer), moved to Rochester.

Short Bros secured a contract to build 35 F.3 and 15 F.5 flying boats designed by John Porte of the Marine Aircraft Experimental Establishment (MAEE) at Felixstowe, the start of the line of development leading to the Empire 'boats. The F 'boats were large aircraft of all-timber construction with fabric-covered flight surfaces. The F.5 was slightly the larger, with a span of 103ft 8in and about one-third of the all-up weight of an Empire 'boat. The wingspan was approaching the 114ft of an Empire 'boat.

Short Bros also set up the airship factory at Cardington in Bedfordshire during the First World War, building two timber-framed Vickers-designed rigid airships, R.31 and R.32, based on German Schutte-Lanz craft, and two duralumin-framed craft, R.37 and R.38, copies of a German Naval Zeppelin. The experience of working in timber and duralumin was to have a far-reaching effect on the future operations of Short Bros and on the whole of the British aircraft industry.

Oswald Short had been experimenting with aluminium alloys for the construction of aircraft by testing light-alloy samples fixed to the jetty piling in the River Medway so that the ebb and flow of the tide alternately exposed them to the water and the air. Opinion at the time was that these alloys had inherent defects and were unsuitable for the primary structures of

aircraft, especially marine aircraft because of corrosion and fatigue. After 36 weeks of dipping in and out of the Medway, it was found the mild steel control samples had virtually rusted away, whereas the alloy samples showed no significant signs of corrosion. Oswald Short's view was that any alleged defects in the light-alloys were because of inadequate manufacturing practices rather than to any inherent defects in the light-alloys themselves.

To prove the point, Short Bros designed and built a small, elegant, single-seat landplane as a private venture. The aircraft was a biplane of all-metal construction and orthodox layout, powered by a 240hp Siddeley Puma engine. The longitudinal stiffeners were cut and fixed between the frames, rather than notching the frames to

ABOVE Shorts F boat. After the war there were many surplus. Short conversion of an F boat showing the 20ft-wide beam with sponsons on both sides. Note the workmanship of the hull. *(Author's collection)*

BELOW Short 310 seaplane outside No 2 Shop at Rochester in about 1916. *(Author's collection)*

allow the longerons to run through continuously. This established a principle of construction, the unnotched frame, which was to be maintained through to the Empire 'boats. The little aircraft, clad in its gleaming alloy skin, was exhibited in 1920 at the Olympia Aero Show, where inevitably it received the name *Silver Streak*.

One of the first jobs for Short Bros' newly employed test pilot, John Lankester Parker (JLP), was to take the *Silver Streak* on its first flight and then to the Royal Aeronautical Establishment at Farnborough to be tested to destruction. RAF pilots had to protest to the Air Ministry before they were allowed to fly the *Silver Streak*, and then only gained permission after receiving official caution. Short Bros were warned not to proceed with light-alloy structures because of what the authorities saw as their inherent dangers, but in

fact the *Silver Streak* established the company as the leading aircraft manufacturer in Europe and the United States. No other manufacturer had the technical expertise demonstrated by the building of this little aeroplane. Shorts proved that they could build stressed-skin structures that resisted cracking and corrosion – opening up the possibility of watertight metal hulls for flying boats.

Horace had died in 1917 (aged only 45), and as Eustace was principally occupied with balloons, Oswald assumed control of the company at Rochester. 'Firm but benevolent' was a description of his control of the company until, 26 years later, it was nationalised under Defence (General) Regulation No 78 in March 1943. Eustace was taught to fly by JLP in 1932 in G-AAFZ, the Short Mussel light seaplane. He had a heart attack at touch down on the Medway opposite the Seaplane Works during a perfect alighting, without time for him to switch the engine off. He was 57. Hugh Oswald Short died in 1969 (aged 86). He had seen the company through the difficult years of the 1920s and early 1930s when, besides designing and building small numbers of aircraft, it had ventured into building Thames barges, lightweight bus bodies, trolley bus bodies, and domestic irons. John Lankester Parker died in 1965.

Imperial Airways Limited (IAL) was formed on 31 March 1924 from the four existing British airlines. In 1936 Short Bros joined with the Belfast shipbuilders Harland and Wolff to form the subsidiary company of Short & Harland Ltd.

Birth of the Empire

Short Bros assigned design index numbers to each project. Design index S.23 was allocated to the new Empire flying boat, followed later by S.30 and S.33. The S.25 was Short Bros' contender for the famous Specification R2/33, which eventually produced the Sunderland. The S.23, S.30, and S.33 'boats had virtually the same outward appearance, differing only in the type of wing float and other minor details.

The S.23 'boats were produced in three Marks: Mk I (the 'standard' 'boat with short-range wings, powered by Bristol Pegasus XC engines, of which 26 were built); Mk II (the 'Bermuda' 'boat with medium-range wings and Pegasus engines, of which two were built); and Mk III (the 'Atlantic' 'boats with long-range wings and Pegasus engines, of which two were built).

The S.30 strengthened 'boats were produced in four Marks: Mk I with Pegasus engines (one built, *Champion*); Mk II, the 'unspecified' 'boat as Mk III (one built, *Australia*); Mk III with long-range wings and Bristol Perseus XIIC engines and flight refuelled hulls (four built); Mk IV, the New Zealand A 'boats with long-range wings and Perseus engines (two built). *Cathay* occupies an ambivalent position in the Empire 'boat family as the last of the S.30s. It was ordered as 'equal to *Champion*' as a 'replacement for *Connemara*'. It is likely, therefore, to have had Pegasus engines.

The two S.33 'hybrid' 'boats (*Clifton* and *Cleopatra*) were built with Bristol Pegasus XIIC engines, strengthened hulls, and medium-range wings. The third, S.33 G-AFRB, was never named and was scrapped in 1943 when 70% complete.

Two S.23M 'boats (*Clio* and *Cordelia*) were converted at Belfast from Mk I S.23 'boats for RAF service, equipped with two Boulton & Paul Type A, four-gun, power-operated turrets – one amidships on the starboard side and the other in the tail. Both 'boats were modified to carry six 430lb internally stowed depth charges. ASV radar completed the conversion. They emerged in March 1941 with RAF serials AX659 and AX660. After AX659 *Clio* crashed at Loch Indal on 22 August 1941, AX660 *Cordelia* was converted back to BOAC wartime standard as G-AEUD.

The impressed QANTAS and TEAL 'boats in Royal Australian Air Force and Royal New Zealand Air Force service were fitted with a variety of armaments. Some 'boats were modified with under-wing bomb racks and transparent plastic cupolas to accommodate No 4 course-setting bombsights in place of mooring hatches. An assortment of 0.303 Lewis guns and 0.5in machine guns on swivel and Scarff mountings were installed in various positions in various 'boats.

Origins and development

The development of the hull of the new Empire flying boat started with the large all-timber F 'boat. Up until the advent of the S.18 'Knuckleduster' in 1933, all the Short 'boats had biplane aerostructures. The 'Knuckleduster' had a monoplane wing and the last developed hull before that of the S.23.

Shorts started their development of the hull with the Cromarty, a developed F 'boat, with a concave planing bottom, resulting in 'cleaner' running on the water and less resistance. The F 'boats, with their flat planing surfaces had a reputation for being somewhat 'dirty' on the water, producing much spray.

In 1924, Shorts built a tiny single-seat flying boat (the S.1 Cockle), and an updated version of the F5 flying boat (the S.2). The Cockle structure was metal, with fabric-covered flight surfaces. The hull was a monocoque, fabricated

BELOW The Cockle motoring along on the Medway with John Lankester Parker in charge, possibly on its first outing on 18 September 1924. JLP tried for 33 minutes to take off, without success. The Rochester landmarks of the Keep and cathedral can be seen on the skyline. *(Author's collection)*

in duralumin, with a flared concave underwater mid-section, transverse main step and second step. The little 'boat was considerably underpowered but was finally flown by JLP for ten minutes on 7 November – the first metal-hulled flying boat in the world to do so. The maximum speed, when it did finally get into the air, was barely 50kts.

The S.2 design was Short Bros' response to the Air Ministry's invitation to tender for two hulls 'of modern design' to suit the aerostructure of the F.5 – still the standard flying boat in service with the RAF. Shorts tendered a developed Cromarty hull, built in duralumin. It was narrower in the beam than the 20ft of the F.3 and F.5, and had a longitudinally fluted planing bottom. The S.2 (RAF serial N177, known in the Service as the 'Tin Five') was mated with a standard biplane F5 aerostructure, and fitted with two Rolls-Royce Eagle VIII engines. It was launched on 31 December 1924 and first flown by John Lankester Parker on 5 January 1925. The S.2 had a span of 103ft 8in, an all-up weight (displacement) of 13,950lb, and a maximum speed of 81kts.

The success of the S.1 and S.2 hulls finally persuaded the Air Ministry that the era of the duralumin hull, even of the all-metal flying boat, had arrived. After the Ministry had ordered six metal-hulled Supermarine Southampton 'boats with displacements of 14,300lb, a bigger 'boat, with a displacement of 21,000lb was designed at Rochester. (Displacements are used here as a measure of the relative sizes of the 'boats.) When submitted to the Air Ministry's Technical Department, this bigger 'boat was rejected in favour of the even larger Blackburn Iris II with a displacement of 27,400lb. Determined not to lose out to the Blackburn 'boat, Oswald Short committed the company to build the new 'boat, and on seeing the drawings for this, Sir Geoffrey Salmon of the Air Council gave a firm order for one aircraft, defined in Specification 13/24. Short Bros' third metal hull was the S.5, named Singapore I, with RAF serial N179.

The Short Bros' design team was led by Francis Webber, and the first scheme for the hull of the new 'boat was based on the patented fluted form of the S.2. This was tested in the William Froude ship tank at the National Physical Laboratory (NPL) at Teddington, which Shorts had been using. However, there are significant differences between the testing of aircraft hulls and ship hulls. Ship hulls tend to be tested at a range of steady speeds. Flying boat hulls exist in a more complex regime; so testing was required for a whole range of characteristics – longitudinal, lateral, and directional stability during take-off and alighting from zero to 70 or 80kts. So, in 1924 Short Bros built their own test tank along the back of No 3 Shop, 300ft long, 6ft wide, 3ft 6in deep, with a capacity of 78,000gal of water, believed to be the first such tank built exclusively for use in the design of aircraft.

When the Rochester test tank was available, the tests were repeated with differing results. The instruments on the Rochester tank were more sensitive, showing the fluted test hull to have increased resistance. Working over the weekend in the Test Department on hull models with fluted and plain underwater bodies, Arthur Gouge and Jack Lower concluded that interference between the multiple bow waves thrown up by the flutes was the source of the increased resistance. In the light of these test runs in the Rochester tank, Francis Webber was asked by Oswald Short – the originator of the idea of arching the planing surfaces – to redesign the hull with an unfluted planing bottom. Webber considered that his design authority had been overruled, took exception to this instruction, and resigned shortly afterwards. Much to his surprise, Arthur Gouge was appointed Chief Designer in his place. The hull of the new 'boat was duly reshaped under his direction, without the flutes or 'arches', thereby establishing a line of hulls running through to the Empire flying boats. At the time of the launch in 1926, S.5 was the largest metal-hulled flying boat in the world, with a displacement of 19,560lb, and the first to be developed in the Rochester testing tank.

Other tests were run to determine the optimum method of providing transverse stability for flying boat hulls. The results were expressed in terms of the load that would have to be sacrificed to get a 'boat off the water using three different methods, wing tip floats, inboard floats, and stub wings or sponsons. Compared to wing tip floats, the loss of load for the inboard floats was 9%, and for the sponsons 14%. Beside the static balance of the aircraft at rest on the water, there were the matters of the engine torque and turning on the water to be considered. Short Bros regarded wing floats to be the safest, lightest, and most economical method available. Retractable floats were rejected as impracticable. The operating mechanism would have to be 100% reliable – something that could not be guaranteed at the time.

The Singapore I is thought to be the first Short Bros aircraft to use a modified version of the Göttingen Gö 436 aerofoil profile for the mainplanes, a thick high-lift aerofoil with low stalling speed, intended for use by monoplanes. This modified Gö 436 profile, known as A.D.5, with varying thickness to chord ratios, became the standard at Rochester. Frise ailerons on set-back hinges were used on the upper mainplanes for the first time.

Sir Alan Cobham and Oswald Short discussed the possibility of a flight to Singapore to demonstrate the capabilities of the flying boat, but finally settled on a tour round the coast of Africa. The Singapore I was loaned by the Air Council to Sir Alan for the journey. It was stripped of its military equipment, cleaned up, repainted, fitted with high-compression Rolls-Royce Condor engines, and registered as G-EBUP on 6 October 1927. The expenses of the expedition were covered by Short Bros and Rolls-Royce as main sponsors, the deficit being made up by Sir Charles Wakefield. The Certificate of Airworthiness for the 'boat in its new form was issued on 7 November 1927 and the 'Sir Charles Wakefield Flight of Survey around Africa' began ten days later. The survey flight was to circumnavigate most of the coast of Africa in a clockwise direction, starting from a landfall at Benghazi on the north coast.

Part of the expedition's route southwards up the River Nile and onwards to Durban, was a preliminary route survey for the projected Imperial Airways Limited service to South Africa.

The flight finished with G-EBUP reverting to N179 in October 1928, and returning to the Seaplane Works at Rochester for modification.

In No 2 Shop, the hull was cut through just forward of the main spar frame bay, a new slice 17in wide inserted, and the whole planing bottom refaired to resemble the hull of the two S.8 Calcutta flying boats then in production next door in No 3 Shop. The Calcuttas were intended to fly the Mediterranean sectors. New engines, Rolls-Royce Buzzards, were installed, and Handley Page auto-slats were fitted to the upper mainplanes. N179 was exhibited at the 7th International Aero Exhibition at Olympia, eight years after the *Silver Streak* made its appearance in the same hall. N179 returned to Felixstowe on 8 November to become the test

ABOVE Singapore I, N179, at the foot of the slipway on 17 August 1926. The public footpath running alongside the River Medway enabled members of the public to watch the launching. This aircraft was loaned to Sir Alan Cobham for his survey flight around Africa. *(Author's collection)*

RIGHT A superb shot of a Short Singapore III, probably K3592, taken in June 1934 on its first flight. K3592 was ferried by 210 Squadron personnel to reinforce 205 Squadron at Singapore, arriving 5 March 1935. *(Author's collection)*

ABOVE Short
Calcutta, G-EBVG,
over the Medway. The
lines of the hull and
planing bottom can
be seen to advantage.
'VG capsized in a
storm at Mirabella,
28 December 1936.
(Shorts)

vehicle for the Rolls-Royce Buzzard engines and the development aircraft for the new Singapore II. The Short Singapore II was developed into the Singapore III, the first of which was on the slipway outside No 3 Shop on 15 June 1934. Production was completed in June 1937, with four more Singapores sharing No 3 Shop with the first 15 Empire 'boats off the line, and the Sunderland prototype.

The Calcutta generally followed the design of the Singapore I, to become the S.8, the first metal-hulled British commercial aircraft with a metal-framed aero structure. The new hull was deeper than that of the Singapore I, with increased beam. The forebody of the hull from the bow to the main step was lengthened to provide the extra buoyancy needed to counter the increased downward thrust of the three engines. The afterbody, aft of the main step, was redesigned so that the tail unit and afterbody were clear of the water at all speeds. The rear step was faired into the afterbody as it swept up to the tail cone, resulting in reduced water resistance and increased aerodynamic advantage. The wing structure was almost identical to the Singapore I, with a small increase in area. IAL's choice of engines was Bristol Jupiter IX nine-cylinder air-cooled radials of 540hp mounted in monocoque nacelles in the gap between the mainplanes, driving four-blade wooden airscrews. Bristol engines were an IAL requirement for the Empire 'boats. Fuel was contained in thickened sections of the upper mainplane, with gravity feed to the engines.

As passengers were to be carried in the new 'boats, no fuel was stored in the hull. This was another precedent that was continued through to the passenger-carrying S.23 Empire 'boats.

The S.16 Scion was a contender for the low cost 5/6-seat commercial aircraft market opened up by the de Havilland DH84 Dragon. The Scion was the first Short Bros aircraft to use the modified Göttingen Gö 436 aerofoil profile on a cantilever monoplane wing, slightly tapered in plan, with rounded tips and inset ailerons. The mainplane spar consisted of two trussed booms, held apart by drag struts top and bottom, to form a box. The boom flanges were cruciform light-alloy extrusions, milled in both dimensions to progressively diminish their area towards the wing tips, corresponding to the spanwise loading on the wing. The spar boom compression members and drag struts were duralumin tubes. An identical structure was used for the main structural members of the tailplane and fin of the Empire 'boats. The principle of the constantly diminishing structural section was used again on the Empire 'boats, whose mainplane structure was finally patented (447 520, 31 May 1935). A wing plan, similar to that of the Scion, was used on the S.18 'Knuckleduster' as the outer mainplane panels.

IAL approached Handley Page Ltd in the spring of 1933 for two additional HP42s as the airline was seriously short of aircraft on their European routes. Handley Page responded with a quotation for a version of the HP42 at double the original price. IAL turned to Short Bros for help, who offered a land version of the S.17 flying boat, to be known as the L.17, named Scylla and Syrinx, using the aerostructure of the S.17s perched on a new fuselage. As time was short, this new fuselage was a heavier braced-frame structure in place of a lighter monocoque, which would have taken longer to design.

The engine nacelles were designed to receive Bristol Jupiter, Pegasus or Perseus engines without modification. The two inboard Jupiters of one of the L.17s were replaced later with Perseus II L sleeve-valve engines, to test their performance in airline conditions. When Syrinx was rebuilt, following an incident in Brussels when it was overturned by a wind gust, it was fitted with four Pegasus XC engines, which by then had been specified for the S.23 Empire

'boats. The passenger accommodation was
a forerunner, almost a prototype, of that used
later for the S.23s.

Short Bros fitted Flettner servo aerofoils to
aircraft with large rudders, to assist in moving
them. Apart from their appearance and other
minor idiosyncrasies, the L.17s had a marked
tendency to wallow in flight. In an attempt to
cure this habit, Scylla was fitted with a modified
rudder early in 1935. The Flettner servo was
removed and a long inset tab – half the height
of the rudder – was built into the trailing edge
in its place. In the event, it was discovered that
a rearward shift of the centre of gravity was a
more effective cure than the inset servo tab, so
the original Flettner servo was replaced.

The S.18 (RAF serial K3574) was a
monoplane, while the other two contenders for
this Specification, the Saro London (K3560) and
the Supermarine Stranraer (K3973), both powered
by Bristol Pegasus engines, were biplanes. These
two aircraft were awarded production contracts.
The Short Bros 'boat was not.

The S.18 was a gull-winged monoplane, the
first Short Bros monoplane flying boat since the
S.1 Cockle, powered by two Rolls-Royce steam-
cooled Goshawk engines, with a displacement
of 18,500lb. To gain tip clearance for the large-
diameter geared-down airscrews, the mainplanes
were cranked upwards at a 30° angle from the
hull to the engines. The knuckle in the mainplane
led inevitably to the nickname 'Knuckleduster'.

Following traditional shipbuilding practice,
the lines of the underwater body and planing
bottom of the hull of the new 'boat were
developed from those of the previous seven
metal hulls. The main step was raked forward
from the centre line of the keel, and the chine
line curved up in a reverse curve as it swept
forward, producing a greater volume forwards
and giving good performance in rough water.
These lines produced a 'boat that ran clean on
the water and was free from porpoising under
normal conditions. The maximum beam was
believed to have been 9ft.

The maximum beam dimension of a flying
boat was the equivalent of the midship section
of a ship, the starting point for the design of
the hull. The accepted practice for deciding the
beam dimension of flying boats was governed
by the so-called 'cube law'. The Rochester

version of the 'law' stated that the beam
dimension (in feet) is equal to 0.36 multiplied by
the cube root of the displacement of the aircraft
on the water in lbs. Short Bros' hulls generally
followed the 'law' up to the Empire hull.

The hull plating of the new 'boat was not swept
inboard above the chine line in the traditional
way, but was straight-sided, with considerable
tumblehome. The hull frames and plating were in
Alclad, with stainless steel fittings used at points
of high stress – characteristics of the hull (except
the tumblehome) later to be incorporated in the
design of the Empire 'boat hulls.

The mainplane construction, too,
foreshadowed that used on the Empire 'boats,
with the modified Gö 436 aerofoil profile. The
wing spar trusses were high-tensile steel tubular
booms, diminishing in gauge and diameter
as the loads decreased towards the tips,
with tubular lift and drag struts, and braced
with tie-rods. The squat cylindrical fuel tanks,
forerunners of those used on the Empire 'boats,
were located between the spar trusses. The
wing floats were carried on vertical struts, which
were sprung with oleo-dampers to absorb
sudden loads while moving on the water.
Lastly, the beaching chassis, and its method of
attachment was an ancestor of the gear used
on the Empire 'boats, and the tail trolley appears
to be identical. An engine and airscrew changing
jib was included in the aircraft's equipment.

A chain of events in 1934 set the scene
for the Empire 'boats. Short Bros received an
outline specification for a four-engined flying

**ABOVE The Mayo
Composite** *Mercury-
Maia*. *(Author's
collection)*

ABOVE The maiden flight of the Short Singapore prototype, with the RAF serial N246, took place on 27 March 1930. Various modifications were made to N246, the most important of which, in the line of ancestry of the Empire 'boats, was the replating of the planing bottom and the revision of the main step. (Shorts)

ABOVE The Short R24/31 'Knuckleduster', K3574, taxiing on the Medway in November 1933. Her high-set Rolls-Royce Goshawk engines are evident. The aircraft is in its original form with unsprung wing tip floats and open tail gunner's position. K3574 was retired in 1938 to become an instructional airframe with the RAF's No 2 School of Technical Training at Cosford. (Shorts)

BELOW The second (of three) Short Kent 'boats, G-ABFB, later named *Sylvanus*, pictured over the Medway on 31 March 1931. 'FB was destroyed by fire at Brindisi on 9 November 1935. (Shorts)

boat from Imperial Airways Limited on 1 May. Shorts' tender for the Empire 'boats was submitted to IAL on 29 June. The first RAF Expansion Scheme 'A' was published on 19 July. The Short–Mayo composite was 'being built', and on 20 December the Empire Air Mail Scheme was announced in principle, followed by an order for 28 Short flying boats.

On 20 October, Oswald Short, Arthur Gouge, and John Parker were at Mildenhall in Suffolk, to watch the start of the MacRobertson Air Race to Australia. Competitor No 44, the first of KLM's Douglas DC-2s, attracted their attention. Competitor No 34, Arthur Hagg's supremely elegant, but tricky to fly, de Havilland DH88 with its tapered wing plan and split flaps, must also have caught their eye. The DH88, registered as G-ACSS and named 'Grosvenor House', was flown by C.W.A. Scott and T. Campbell Black to win the race in 70hr 54min and the prize of £15,000. Competitor No 44, the specially adapted airliner carrying passengers who had paid 5,000 guilders each for the privilege of the return flight finished second, 19hr 9min after SS Grosvenor House. The visit of the Shorts' Rochester management to Mildenhall confirmed their conviction that the day of the biplane was well and truly over. The Scion had been flying for 16 months and the 'Knuckleduster' for 11 months, both monoplanes. The first sketches of the Short S.22, the Scion Senior, yet another monoplane, must have been on the drawing boards at Rochester. The half-sized flying precursor of the Empire 'boats, the Scion Senior, had a wing plan that was doubled up for the Empires.

The inspiration for the design of the Empire flying boats undoubtedly came from Arthur Gouge, the General Manager and Chief Designer at Rochester. He was ably supported by the two Assistant Chief Designers – Messrs C.P.T. Lipscomb and W.C. Jackson – and by Mr W. Browning, the Head of Stress Office. At Short Bros' Annual General Meeting in November 1936, Oswald Short paid a handsome tribute to Arthur Gouge, saying that he carried the greatest responsibility for the design of the new 'boat and that the greatest credit should go to him. The major decisions committing the company to the project were, however, taken by Oswald Short.

The development of the Empire 'boat hull started with the Cromarty, with its concave planing bottom. It continued through the Cockle, the world's first metal-hulled flying boat, the Singapore I and II, the Calcutta, the Singapore III, with its raked forward main step, the stately Sarafand, the second largest flying boat of its day, the Kent 'boats, and finally the 'Knuckleduster'. Mainplane development started with the adoption and modification of the Göttingen Gö 436 aerofoil, probably on the Singapore I. The cantilevered monoplane wing was first used on the Scion, developed further for the Scion Senior and the 'Knuckleduster', and ultimately for the Empire, Sunderland, and Stirling wings. The highly effective Gouge flaps were tried out on the modified mainplane of the DR Scion II, flying as M3. The fuel tanks installed between the spars in the mainplanes of the Empire 'boats first appeared in the 'Knuckleduster'. The Frise ailerons were first used on the Singapore I; the Bristol air-cooled radial engines on the Calcutta; the quick-release hook near the tail on the Kents; and the engine changing jib, the rudiments of the beaching chassis, and the tail trolley on the 'Knuckleduster'. The rudder servo tab was tried on Scylla. Like the L.17s, the Empire 'boats could carry a spare engine.

ABOVE **First of the Empires – Canopus.** *(Author's collection)*

The Empire Flying-boat

NEW LINERS FOR IMPERIAL AIRWAYS

A fleet of high-speed *Empire* air liners and flying-boats is under construction; they will be even more comfortable than the existing liners and will be equipped with sleeping berths and will have two decks

INSURANCE

Imperial Airways is the only air transport company in the world in which the personal accident assurance rates are the same as for surface travel

INCLUSIVE TOUR RATES

When arranging holiday or business tours, ask your travel agent about the special quotations for travelling by air to almost any city in Europe. These rates include hotel accommodation, and you will be surprised how little such journeys will cost you

NO TIPS—WHAT A SAVING

There are NO TIPS to pay on Imperial Airways' services, either on its European or Empire routes, and a passenger only has to reckon what he normally spends on tips on a journey to, say, Calcutta, to realise how advantageous this is to him

FAR LEFT *Canopus* sits on the waters of the Medway beside a Singapore III, while overhead flies the second of the Empires, *Caledonia*. *(Author's collection)*

LEFT **New aircraft for Imperial Airways – the Empire 'boats.** *(Author's collection)*

Chapter Two

The 'C' class in service

Surprisingly, the colourful operational life of the Empire 'boats spanned little more than a decade, carrying mail and passengers to the furthermost corners of the British Empire. Their flying career embraced first the Empire Air Mail Programme and, with the onset of the Second World War, the Horseshoe Route from England to South Africa.

OPPOSITE *Canopus* **out-shopped at Rochester after interior fitment.** *(Author's collection)*

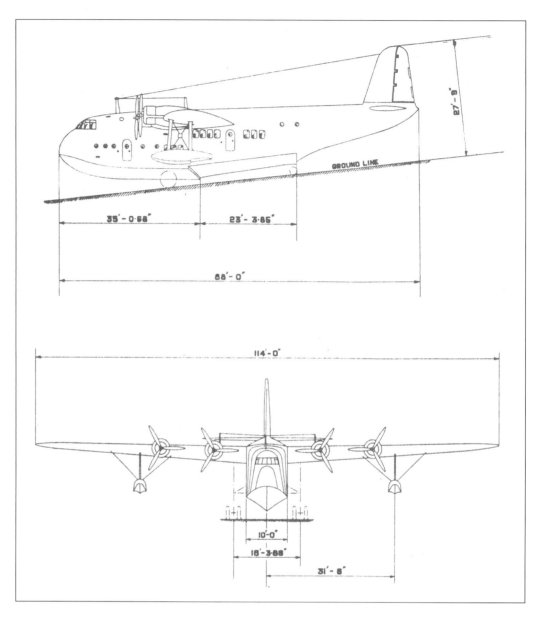

The 'C' class

The design and construction of the new 'boats proceeded in secrecy, and the first illustration of an Empire 'boat available to the public is believed to have been on the front cover of Short Bros' 1935 annual report.

The Empire flying boats were all given names starting with the letter 'C', and all were initially taken on the UK register. The choice of 'C' as the class initial for the Empire 'boats was an accident of the alphabet. Later the six

Australian QANTAS 'boats and the two New Zealand TEAL 'boats were transferred to the national registers of those countries, with the exception of *Australia* which remained on the British register. The two New Zealand 'boats had their names changed to *Awarua* and *Aotearoa*.

The operational history of the Empire 'boats is in two unequal parts, divided by the outbreak of the Second World War in 1939. The first part was the Empire Air Mail Scheme (EAMS), which on 29 June 1937 was renamed the Empire Air Mail Programme (EAMP), and the second part was flying the Horseshoe Route and becoming involved with the conduct of the war.

THIS PAGE The roll-out before launch of *Canopus* (the as yet unnamed G-ADHL) on the famous slipway outside No 3 Erecting Shop at the Seaplane Works, Rochester. The figure in the left foreground (top picture) must surely be H.O. Short, admiring the company's handiwork. *(Shorts)*

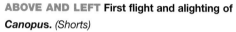

ABOVE AND LEFT First flight and alighting of
***Canopus.** (Shorts)*

The Empire Air Mail Scheme

The British government announced its approval of the Empire Air Mail Scheme (EAMS) on 20 December 1934, which was to improve and expand communications by carrying all letter mail within the Empire and the Dominions without surcharge. Imperial Airways Limited (IAL) was to operate the service, flying two new aircraft, the Short four-engined flying boats ('C' class) and the Armstrong Whitworth AW27 land planes ('E' class). The 'E' class were to fly IAL's European sectors and the better-developed eastern route as far as Calcutta. The flying boats ('C' class Empire) were to fly the remainder of the routes.

Besides IAL, the other two companies that eventually came together to operate the service were the Australian airline QANTAS (Queensland and Northern Territories Air Service) formed in 1920 – the second oldest airline in the world – and Tasman Empire Airways Limited (TEAL).

LEFT S.30 Empire 'boat G-AFCY, *Awarua*, went to TEAL in March 1940 as ZK-AMC. *(British Airways Speedbird Heritage Centre)*

TEAL, the New Zealand component of the new air service was a partnership, formed in 1940, between the New Zealand government, Union Airways, BOAC, and QANTAS.

The estimated requirement for the Empire Air Mail Scheme was for 26 flying boats and two spares, with a service life of ten years, and a replacement aircraft needed in service by 1944. Short Bros received 'Instructions to proceed' from IAL dated 1 January 1935, and the original construction order, dated 19 February 1935, was for two flying boats (the 'prototype' and 'one for Bermuda'). Subsequent orders covered the remainder of the production. From the start of design of the first 'boat to first flight took about 108 weeks.

The Empire routes to South Africa and Australia were subject to extremes of weather, with existing airfields prone to flooding by monsoon rain and to wind damage. The Handley Page HP42 ('H' class), already in service with an all-up weight of 28,000lb, was thought to be the heaviest land aircraft able to operate from many of the small grass airfields along the routes. The existing Armstrong Whitworth AW XV Atalantas ('A' class), with all-up weights of 12,000lb, flying in partnership with the HP42s, had been specially designed for the hot and high sectors of the South African route. The new aircraft for the EAMP would be considerably heavier than either, and as they were expected to weigh over 40,000lb many of the existing aerodromes would require costly improvements, such as hard-surfaced runways, to bring them up to standard. The partners of the Empire 'boats on the EAMP – the Armstrong Whitworth AW27 Ensign landplanes ('E' class) – had all-up weights of up to 55,500lb. They were intended to operate over those parts of the routes that already had airports with established facilities.

The choice of flying boats for the main Empire routes was based on a number of assumptions. IAL was already operating the Short Calcutta and Kent flying boats on the Mediterranean and African sectors, so had previous experience of running a maritime fleet. Sir Alan Cobham's successful tour of Africa in Short Singapore I G-EBUP (including some route-proving flying southwards up the Nile) was another factor in favour of the flying boat.

ABOVE Imperial Airways poster (1936) for one of the '28 new 200 miles an hour two-decker Empire flying-boats'. *(British Airways Speedbird Heritage Centre)*

The EAMP routes, although they crossed some difficult ground and were subject to extremes of the weather, were largely in existence and over friendly territory – and for the most part they were over water. The four engines specified for the new flying boats would enable the aircraft to maintain height should an engine fail while over land. If an emergency should occur over water, a flying boat had a good chance of alighting successfully and remaining afloat until help

ABOVE G-AETY,
Clio, alongside at
Marseilles-Marignane
flying-boat terminal in
the South of France.
(Author's collection)

arrived. The establishment of marine airports, with sufficient alternative alighting areas, appeared to be feasible and low in capital cost. Some investment, however, would be required by way of port and radio facilities. Some 8 British Power Boat attendant surface craft had been delivered to IAL by October 1936, and 30 more were on order. Some smaller Sea Rover 22ft launches were also on order.

The primary function of both the new 'E' and 'C' class aircraft was to carry EAMP and government mail within the Empire. The standard Mk I S.23 flying boats were specified to carry 1,500kg of mail and freight and 24 passengers at a cruising speed of 130kts for 435 nautical miles against a headwind of 35kts. Payload not required for mail was available for freight and passengers. The seemingly short-range requirement was based partly on the structure of the routes and on the assumption that alternative alighting areas would be available. The specified range was found to be insufficient in some weather conditions over India in the monsoon season. If Lake Bracciano (the port for Rome) was shrouded in cloud, the Mk I S.23 'boats did not have enough range to return to Marseilles, so an alternative alighting area was later arranged on Lake Paola, between Rome and Naples. Lastly, the cost of fuel at ports on the seaboard was likely to be half that at inland airfields in the remoter parts of the world.

At the time of their inception in 1934, the Empire flying boats were expected to have an operational life of not more than ten years, but at the end of 1944 16 of the 42 Empire 'boats built were still flying – eleven S.23s, four S.30s, and one S.33. Some of them were slightly battered and worn, but they were still giving good service.

From 1 November 1938, all British transport aircraft were required to have some means of airframe de-icing. Airframe and airscrew icing caused some difficulties in winter, especially on the overland sectors across France. IAL began using Kilfrost – a newly developed glycol-based anti-icing paste. This was applied by brush or palette knife to the leading edges of the vital parts of the airframe, the mainplanes, aerial mast, fin and tailplanes, and the struts and noses of the wing tip floats. It was, though, only partially effective because of problems with adhesion, its tendency to corrode metal, and it being abraded by heavy rain and hail. It was also possible for ice to form on the surface of the Kilfrost itself. The intention was to fit Goodrich pulsating rubber 'overshoes' to the leading edges of the wing and tail surfaces of *Clyde*, one of the S.30 'boats. The S.23 'boats did not originally have de-icing devices for the airscrews, but some were subsequently fitted with full or partial equipment – a mixture of old Dunlop slinger rings and the latest de Havilland equipment. When the two 'boats were converted to S.23M status they were equipped with the full airframe de-icing kit.

Empire routes were already in existence in varying degrees of readiness. (The names of the countries referred to are those in use at the time the EAMP was in operation.) Outbound from the United Kingdom, the routes were common across Europe to the Kingdom of Egypt, where they branched. One route stretched southwards to terminate at Durban in the Dominion of South Africa. The other lay eastwards from Egypt across the Middle East, Palestine, India, Burma, the Malaysian Straits Settlements, and the Dutch East Indies to Australia. The Antipodean service was later extended from Brisbane to Sydney and finally across the Tasman Sea to Auckland, New Zealand. A potentially lucrative tourist service between New York and Bermuda was run in pool with Pan American Airlines until *Cavalier* was caught by carburettor icing and forced down over the Atlantic on 21 January 1939. This route was considered to be important as the 'Bermuda flying boat' was the second 'C' class 'boat ordered.

A 'water aerodrome' – an area of Southampton Water, one mile long by 400 yards wide off the Royal Victoria Hospital – had already been declared to be the Empire Air Scheme Terminal, marked 'Aircraft night landing [*sic*] marked by movable lights'. Not withstanding the marked terminal area, some of the 'boats took off in daylight as and where they could, which caused some dismay and consternation to the pilots and masters of the ocean-going liners and other shipping plying the Water, who considered the flying boats to be trespassing on their exclusive domain. The maintenance base was opposite the Terminal in the former Vickers-Supermarine works at Hythe.

Empires at war

At the outbreak of the Second World War on 3 September 1939, IAL's operations were moved from Southampton Water to Poole Harbour to avoid the barrage balloons and anti-aircraft artillery defending Southampton. But the 'boats were still serviced at the engineering base at Hythe. Irrespective of 'the colours of the day' signal, they ran the risk of being fired on by anti-aircraft guns as they flew in for maintenance.

The 'boats were particularly vulnerable to mishap while on the water. On its delivery flight to the Mediterranean in October 1936, *Canopus* (Major H.G. Brackley, Captain F.J. Bailey, First Officer S. Long, Radio Officer Bell, Flight Clerk Adams, and Steward Doyle), en route for Bordeaux and Marignane, was in danger of being overwhelmed by the Seine bore after bad weather had forced an alighting at Caudebec in

ABOVE A moody image of an Empire 'boat moored on the River Nile as the sun begins to set. *(British Airways Speedbird Heritage Centre)*

LEFT Durban in South Africa was the main base for the Horseshoe Route and hosted a major Imperial Airways flying boat maintenance facility. *(Shutterstock)*

RIGHT G-ADUV,
Cambria (Captain
L.A. Egglesfield), flew
a survey flight from
Alexandria to Durban
in May 1937 loaded
with Air Ministry
radio equipment for
the ground stations
along the East
African coastline at
Lindi, Mozambique,
Quilemane, and
Beira. The equipment
was installed as it
went. *(British Airways
Speedbird Heritage
Centre)*

northern France. This was the first occasion that
an Empire 'boat had met a river bore. Captain
Bailey was uncertain whether to breast the
advancing wave while taxiing to meet it, or to
moor up and take the necessary precautions to
prevent the aircraft charging the mooring buoy,
as the tail was lifted by the passing wave front.
The aircraft remained moored and the 'boat
rode the bore without difficulty.

Cambria (Captain G.J. Powell) was
disabled at Toronto on 28 August 1937 before
thousands of spectators around the lake who
were watching the alighting when the port
wing float struck a semi-submerged log on the
surface. The log tore jagged holes in the float
and *Cambria* took a list to port as crew and
passengers scrambled up the upper surface
of the starboard mainplane to balance it. A
spare float and fittings were dispatched from
Rochester and brought across the Atlantic on
RMS *Berengaria*. *Cambria* was out of action
for a month, arriving back at Foynes on
28 September at 08:14 BST after a flight of
10hr 36min, the shortest of the five survey
flights, at an average speed of 165kts.

Coorong was driven ashore while at
moorings in Darwin Harbour on 12 December
1938. A squall blew up, gusting to 48kts and

RIGHT After *Cambria*
(Captain G.J. Powell)
was disabled
alighting at Toronto
on 28 August 1937
before thousands
of spectators, a
spare wing float and
other fittings were
dispatched from
Rochester and brought
across the Atlantic on
the White Star–Cunard
liner RMS *Berengaria*.
(TopFoto)

building up the biggest sea ever seen in the harbour. The 3in Manila line securing the 'boat broke at 21:03. Although screwed right home and secured with wire in the normal way for a night stop, the storm pennant shackle (attached to a ring on the buoy) worked loose. *Coorong,* with four engineers and a watchman on board, broke loose and was driven ashore, fetching up with the hull fast across a timber jetty, with the starboard mainplane overhanging a low cliff. Those on board escaped along the starboard wing to dry land. The planing bottom was gashed on the starboard side between Frames 5 and 8. During the storm, the sea was breaking over the coupé, and under the mainplanes. The aft freight hatch burst open. The rescue party worked to hold the aircraft, securing it with ropes to a nearby lamp-post. They earthed up under the starboard mainplane, and then lay on the top of the starboard wing to weigh it down to stop the pounding. Later, baulks of timber and steel roofing sheet were piled on the mainplane to hold it in position. To prevent the jetty collapsing under the weight of the aircraft, extra steelwork was welded in position before the next high tide. *Coorong* was dismantled and returned to Rochester for rebuilding, starting in May 1939. The 'boat was back in service on 14 November 1939, having being out of service for nearly 11 months.

The 'boats also had to contend with the 'suds' of the Nile (floating islands of papyrus and elephant grass weighing tons), semi-submerged hippopotami in Lake Victoria, and crocodiles that liked to swallow the orange-coloured rubber mooring buoys. Also, miscellaneous flotsam (up to and including whole trees) abounded in the rivers. One such nearly sank *Cooee* (Captain F.J. Bailey) on the River Congo at Leopoldville on the flight out from the UK to reinforce the Horseshoe Route. During the night, a white signal flare fired from the 'boat brought the launch out in the pouring rain. A 60ft-long tree lay across *Cooee*'s mooring line. Either the mooring line would snap and the 'boat whirl away downriver in the darkness, or the tree would break loose and stave in the hull. Captain Bailey started the engines while the launch party tried to drag the tree away. At each attempt, the towing line round the tree broke. A steam tug was called

but it could not move the tree either. At dawn, the mooring line was cut, hoping that the 'boat would drift away faster than the tree. Captain Bailey managed to swing the 'boat clear as the tree swept by.

Some river alighting areas used by the 'boats were subject to exceptionally strong currents, making handling on the water difficult. Allahabad was one at the confluence of the Jumna and Ganges rivers, with the river current normally running at 7kts but increasing to 14kts on occasions. The alighting area at Calcutta on the River Hooghly near the Howrah Bridge was another, with the river running full of eddies and undercurrents, making taxiing difficult.

On 10 August 1939, *Australia* ran aground at Basra prior to taking off, bound for Singapore with 12 passengers on board. *Australia* was turning in the narrow channel when it was allowed to run hard aground on Coal Island at considerable speed. The bow was stove

BELOW Empire 'boats were frequent visitors to the River Nile in the thirties and forties. *(Shutterstock)*

BOTTOM Floating 'suds' (seen here in the foreground) were a constant hazard to flying boats on the Nile. Here, apparently untroubled by the clump of floating vegetation, G-AETW, *Calpurnia* **is replenished with engine oil. She was later to crash on Lake Habbaniyah on 27 November 1938.** *(British Airways Speedbird Heritage Centre)*

in, the skin plating buckled back to Frame 9 on the port side and the keelson fractured at Frame 2. The port float became detached, the extreme edge of the port flap was damaged, and the port aileron slightly damaged. The 'boat became submerged to the underside of the mainplanes, and had to be lifted clear of the water by barge crane. The damage was repaired by rebuilding the forward part of the 'boat on the bank, before the aircraft was flown back to the UK. The aircraft was unserviceable

for two months before being renamed *Clare* and put back in service.

In February 1941, *Clyde* was employed on the West African Poole–Lagos service, moored on the River Tagus at Lisbon, ready for the expected service to the UK. At 05:00 the flight was cancelled because of the weather. By 09:00 the wind had reached Force 8, and by 10:00 the aircraft was adrift. Attempts to anchor the aircraft succeeded when the anchor finally held about 100 yards north-east of Sacor Pier. Although the locking pin of the bolt of the mooring shackle was secured, the bolt (made of normalised BSS 3.S.6 40-ton steel) fractured and the aircraft slipped its moorings. The storm, which was the worst experienced since 1854, continued unabated. At 15:30 Captain F.D. Travers attempted to board *Clyde* with the intention of taxiing back to the original mooring, but he was prevented by the sea that was then running. At 16:45 the port wing float was punctured by debris and the port mainplane gradually submerged. The sea was breaking right over the aircraft, and at 17:00 a gust under the starboard mainplane capsized the 'boat. It hovered for a minute upright in the water, before settling on its back at an angle of 50°. After firing two red signal lights, two of the three men on board jumped clear. One preferred to stay with the 'boat and was unfortunately drowned. The BOAC staff were assisted by PAA personnel, who considered that a Boeing 314 would not have been able to withstand such weather conditions for more than an hour. By 18:00, all that could be seen was the aft part of the hull, forward to the freight compartment porthole. The hull was lying inverted at an angle of 25°. On this occasion some parts of the aircraft were salvaged and the remains written off.

The only significant air strikes recorded were encounters with birds and lightning. *Aotearoa* collided with a vulture over India on its delivery flight to New Zealand on 19 August 1939, the bird hitting the windscreen at a closing speed of 170kts without damage to the aircraft. A flight of 50 geese damaged the leading edge of the mainplane of another 'boat. *Canopus* was struck by lightning while flying near Corfu, and *Aotearoa* was struck while over the Tasman Sea in June 1941, causing a fire on the control deck.

The Second World War brought other hazards arising from military action. *Clare* was

nearly set on fire by an incendiary bomb at moorings in Kalafrana Harbour, Malta. The bomb penetrated the top of the hull and set alight some of the seats. The fire was extinguished. This was some seven months before *Clare* succumbed to an engine fire over the Atlantic between Bathurst and Lisbon.

The most common man-made incidents were collisions with the array of attendant surface craft, particularly refuelling barges and control tenders. *Champion* was hit by a felucca cast adrift on the Nile by young boys, and Sunderland JM 722 broke loose during a gale, to collide with *Coorong*'s port mainplane and tail-plane. A submarine was encountered by a 'boat while taxiing in Naples Harbour. The hull plating on another 'boat, *Cordelia*, was torn while a beaching leg was being attached as the 'boat swung in the choppy water.

The 'boats themselves sometimes caused collisions. One broke away from its moorings on Southampton Water and collided with a yacht, ending up with the tailplane entangled in the rigging. On another occasion *Champion* collided with a hospital ship while taxiing in Durban Harbour, grazing the hull with a wing tip and carrying away some staging being used to paint the ship's hull. *Carpentaria* met head-on *Peng Am 46,* a two-masted junk, staving in the nose of the starboard float, bending the starboard outer airscrew, and tearing out part of the leading edge of the mainplane.

Empires in decline

At the end of January 1945 it was decided that the Empire 'boats would not be converted back to the pre-war standard passenger accommodation. The time limit on the Empire 'boat mainplane spars was set at 13,250 flying hours. It is not clear if this figure was decided when the 'boats were designed, as a limit to their operational lives, or whether it was imposed at a later date. By 31 May 1945, *Canopus* had 12,794hr on the logbook and there were four more of the surviving 'boats with similar hours. In the final reckoning, when they came to be scrapped, four of the BOAC 'boats had exceeded the limit with more than 15,000hr, and one had 14,989hr.

On 17 October 1946*, Canopus* (Captain H.L.

Fry) arrived back in the United Kingdom for the last time. A week and a day later *Canopus* was handed over for scrapping – after a service life of ten years with 15,026 hours on the log. The first was followed by the last. By the end of the month, the last of the Empire 'boats to be launched, *Cleopatra* (10,513 hours), had arrived back and was scrapped on 4 November 1946.

When the end came, of the 16 'boats that survived the war, 13 were reduced to 'produce' at Hythe, one in Sydney and two at Auckland. *Cathay* was offered to the Science Museum in London for preservation but regretfully the museum declined because of storage difficulties, as it had itself been bombed.

On 12 March 1947 *Caledonia* departed Durban for Southampton for the last time, closing the Horseshoe Route. The schedule on the file recording the return of the surviving Empire 'boats to the UK for scrapping has a pencil note in the margin reading: 'the end of an era'.

In New Zealand, *Aotearoa* and *Awarua* were withdrawn from service in October 1946 to be scrapped. The longest-serving Empire 'boat, *Coriolanus*, was withdrawn from service in Sydney and scrapped in December 1947.

ABOVE This beautiful image of G-AFCT, *Champion,* shows the 'boat at anchor on the Nile in the early war period. Note the Imperial Airways crew on the jetty (wearing tropical kit) and the BOAC Speedbird emblem suspended from the roof of the building in the foreground. *(Author's collection)*

Chapter Three

Spanning the globe

At their peak in the late thirties, Imperial Airways' 'C' class Empire flying boats flew a route network that linked Britain with the Middle East, India, Hong Kong, Malaya, South Africa, Australia, and New Zealand. Fares were all-inclusive and the airline prided itself on offering a service with 'no tips and no extras'.

OPPOSITE The Pacific waters lap gently against the hull of Empire 'boat *Castor* as it is refuelled from the Shell Aviation Services tender at Gladstone in Queensland. This Australian port was a flying boat stop on the Horseshoe Route south towards the New South Wales coast and the EAMS terminus at Sydney, where the 'boats would alight on the harbour at Rose Bay. G-ADUW *Castor* was a special Empire 'boat. It had the highest utilisation time logged in Imperial Airways/ BOAC records at 15,789 hours, representing a total distance flown of about 2.2 million nautical miles (or 4 million km). *(Author's collection)*

The Empire Air Mail Scheme route

It was intended that the EAMS route be flown by a partnership of the Armstrong Whitworth AW.27 land planes and the Short S.23 flying boats, but this was compromised by the late delivery of the AW.27s, victims of the rearmament programme and a constant stream of modifications from IAL. The first of the AW.27s, G-ADSR *Ensign* (maiden flight 24 January 1938), was delivered two years late. The service lives of the 'E' class were fraught with difficulties. They had to be recalled twice for up-rated engines to be installed, which put a considerable strain on the whole of IAL's operations. The Empire flying boats, which were delivered nearly on time, took practically the whole strain of flying the EAMS.

IAL's operations on the European and Empire routes were divided into Areas and the aircraft allotted to the four numbered Operating Divisions. A new Division, No 5 Division, was formed to operate the Empire 'boats. The Division grew in size as the 'boats were progressively delivered from Rochester, until it finally absorbed Nos 2, 3, and 4 Divisions to be named the Empire Division.

Early in 1935, an Air Mail Division was formed in the Foreign Section of the General Post Office (GPO) in London to handle the outbound mail from all origins in the United Kingdom. More than half the airmail in the United Kingdom originated in London, posted in special blue-painted airmail letterboxes. One surviving blue airmail letterbox stands on the corner of High Street and St Albans Street in Windsor. The mail was collected in matching blue-painted 'streamlined' Morris vans.

Outbound mail was divided into 'roads', each road representing a destination, a country or group of countries, rather than a route. The mail was sorted at the General Post Office in London for road, 68% for the EAMS, 26% for European destinations and 6% for other countries, and then made up into mails. Outbound EAMS mail was dispatched to Southampton by train, to begin its journey to the Empire and Dominions. Each mail was identified by the road and direction. The roads were A Africa and I India, which extended to Singapore, and eventually, Sydney. The direction of the service was indicated by W for westbound mails, inbound to the UK, E for outbound to India and beyond, and S and N for the southbound and northbound services to and from Africa. The North Atlantic services were coded NAW or NAE, depending on direction. Each mail carried a serial number.

The GPO contract required IAL to deliver the mail within 24 hours of the scheduled arrival time for full payment. A delivery within 48 hours of the scheduled time was paid at half rate, and if the mail was later than 48 hours, IAL carried the mail for nothing.

At the start of the EAMS, the two main Empire routes were already largely in operation, part rail, and flown by a mixture of landplanes and flying boats. Outbound from the United Kingdom, the routes were common to the

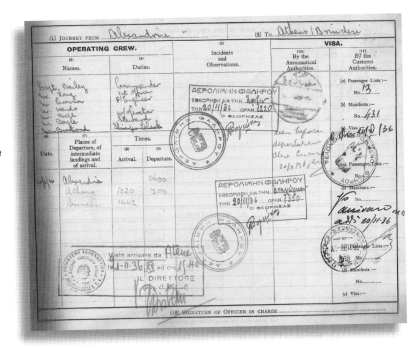

Kingdom of Egypt (place and country names in this account are recorded as they were at the time) where they branched.

The first EAMS mail was flown by G-ADHL Canopus (Captain F.J. Bailey) – then IAL's one and only Empire 'boat – on 30 October 1936, less than two years after the announcement of the Scheme. Canopus lifted the 490th inbound India Westbound mail (IW 490) from Alexandria to Brindisi, from where it went by train to Paris and then forward by air to London.

The African arm of the EAMS stretched southwards to terminate at Durban in the Dominion of South Africa. The other arm lay eastwards from Egypt across the Middle East, Palestine, India, Burma and the Malaysia Straits Settlements, and the Dutch East Indies, and eventually to Australia. The Antipodean service was later extended from Brisbane to Sydney and finally across the Tasman Sea to Auckland, New Zealand. Both routes were about 19% longer than their respective great circle distances.

EAMS flying boat operations on Southampton Water started on 13 December 1936 when Centaurus departed with India Eastbound (IE 505) mail for Alexandria. Centaurus then joined Canopus in the Mediterranean, as IAL's second revenue-earning Empire 'boat. Caledonia joined in the effort to move the Christmas mails, and demonstrated its long-range performance by taking 5,588kg

ABOVE **Page from the logbook** *of Canopus* **recording a flight from Alexandria to Athens and Brindisi on 20–21 November 1936.** *(British Airways Speedbird Heritage Centre)*

RIGHT 'UZ *Cygnus* crashed in Brindisi Harbour during take-off. The aircraft was westbound at the time of the accident, carrying passengers – including Air Marshal Sir John Salmond (a director of Imperial Airways) and Robert Lutyens, the architect son of Sir Edwin – and mail. The captain and first officer were unhurt but the radio officer and five of the passengers, including Sir John and Robert Lutyens, were injured and one passenger and the steward, killed. The crash was attributed to the Captain losing control owing to a problem caused by the wing flaps. *(British Airways Speedbird Heritage Centre)*

of mail from Southampton to Alexandria, via Marseilles and Brindisi. The fifth delivery from the Seaplane Works in Rochester, *Castor*, was launched and delivered before the end of 1936, bringing the fleet at the end of the year to two Mk Is and one Mk II on the UK to Alexandria route, one Mk III 'Atlantic' 'boat, and the other Mk II in Bermuda.

The introduction of the EAMS proceeded apace. In January 1937, the rail terminal was diverted from Brindisi to Marseilles. On 1 January, *Centaurus* arrived at Marseilles from Alexandria with AN 407 mail, inaugurating the Marseilles to Alexandria sectors of the route. The three S.23 'boats maintained the Mediterranean service until the beginning of February 1938 when a scheduled two-day service from Hythe to Alexandria started.

RIGHT Page from the logbook *of Canopus* recording a flight from Southampton to Marseilles on 16–17 April 1937. *(British Airways Speedbird Heritage Centre)*

TYPICAL FLIGHT SCHEDULE TO ALEXANDRIA

London (Waterloo)	depart	by train 19:30 (all times local)
Southampton station	arrive	21:28 (night stop)
Southampton	depart	05:15
Marseilles	arrive	12:25
Rome	arrive	16:15 (night stop)
Rome	depart	07:15
Brindisi	depart	10:00
Athens	depart	14:10
Alexandria	arrive	19:00 (night stop)

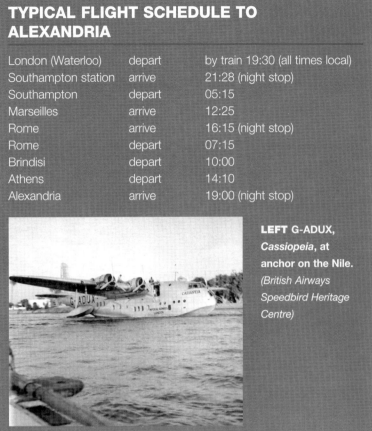

LEFT G-ADUX, *Cassiopeia*, at anchor on the Nile. *(British Airways Speedbird Heritage Centre)*

ABOVE **The cover of a guide booklet issued to Imperial Airways flying boat passengers in 1938.** *(British Airways Speedbird Heritage Centre)*

The first through-service from Southampton to Alexandria was flown by *Cassiopeia* (Captain G.J. Powell) on 26 January 1937, taking 13 passengers and 762kg of AS 417 mail. The cross flight was made by *Castor* bringing in AN 416 mail on 4 February 1937. The regular service had begun with four S.23 'boats.

Castor (Captain H.W.C. Alger) inaugurated the eastbound service on 6 February 1937, taking off at 11:47 with eight passengers and 1,250kg of IE 521 mail (some of which was to go forward to Australia), only to return with oiled spark plugs at 12:11. Hundreds of spectators, some of whom had been brought in by four special trains from London, witnessed the event that demonstrated some of the difficulties with which the IAL crews had to contend. 'Castor oiled' was one newspaper comment. Bad weather set in, so *Castor* did not get away until 8 February.

An agreement between Great Britain and Australia, lasting 15 years, consented to the use of the Empire 'boats. Either side had the right to terminate the agreement within two years and withdraw, should the aircraft prove unsatisfactory.

On 18 February 1937, *Caledonia* flew direct from Hythe to Alexandria in 13hr 44min at an average speed of 148kts. *Cavalier*, the Bermuda 'boat had been knocked down in crates and dispatched by ship to Bermuda. It was assembled at IAL's base on Darrel Island and was test flown the next day.

Regular two-day services between the UK and Egypt began on 24 February 1937. The last westbound Empire service to be flown by a land aircraft arrived at Croydon Airport from Africa at 11:45 on 4 March 1937. The next day, IAL opened the base at Hythe on Southampton Water. *Capella* departed with IE 528 mail, and from that day onwards all the EAMS mail outbound and inbound to Southampton was flown by the Empire 'boats. The mail was trans-shipped at Cairo into land aircraft for the remainder of its journey, eastwards or southwards.

THIS PAGE 'UU *Cavalier*, the Mk II 'Bermuda boat', was dismantled and shipped to Bermuda in packing cases before being offloaded and towed to Darrel Island, the joint Pan Am/Imperial Airways flying boat base. On the single-sector New York–Bermuda service, *Cavalier* could carry a full complement of 24 passengers. An assistant steward was carried in place of the flight clerk. *(British Airways Speedbird Heritage Centre)*

EMPIRE FLYING BOAT SERVICES OF IMPERIAL AIRWAYS AND ASSOCIATED COMPANIES 1936

Service frequency

4 services a week	England–Greece–Egypt
2 services a week	England–East Africa–South Africa
	England–India–Malaya–Australia
1 service a week	England–Hong Kong
	England–Nigeria (Mails only at present)

Sample fares

London to	Single	Return
Cairo	£42 (£1,553)	£75 12s (£2,795) [£2,953]
Calcutta	£108 (£3,993)	£194 (£7,188) [£5,504]
Johannesburg	£125 (£4,662)	£225 (£8,320) [£4,698]
Nairobi	£109 (£4,030)	£196 (£7,248) [£6,109]
Rangoon	£120 (£4,437)	£216 (£7,987)
Singapore	£156 (£5,768)	£280 (£10,354) [£7,249]
Hong Kong	£175 (£6,471)	£315 (£11,648) [£7,688]
Brisbane	£160 (£5,916)	£288 (£10,650) [£9,926]
Alexandria to Karachi	£50 (£1,849)	£90 (£3,328)
Karachi to Singapore	£71 (£2,625)	£127 16s (£4,726)

Fares include all transport, food, and hotel accommodation (passengers sleep on land each night).
No tips and no extras.
Fares based on weight of 221lb including passengers' baggage. Excess at low rates.
Special rates for British officers and certain government officials.

Key
(The UK National Archives currency converter http://www.nationalarchives.gov.uk/currency tells you how much yesterday's money was worth in 2005. For example, in 1935, £288 0s 0d would have the same spending worth of £10,650.24 in 2005 – the latest date for comparison currently available.)
[The cost of a British Airways first-class return flight, September 2012]

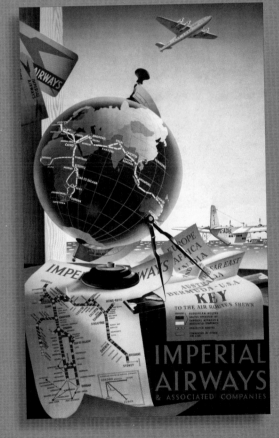

ABOVE An Imperial Airways poster illustrating the airline's global route network. *(British Airways Speedbird Heritage Centre)*

ABOVE Juba, the capital of South Sudan, with the River Nile on the right. *(Shutterstock)*

ABOVE RIGHT The cover of a guide booklet issued to Imperial Airways flying boat passengers travelling the Africa route. *(British Airways Speedbird Heritage Centre)*

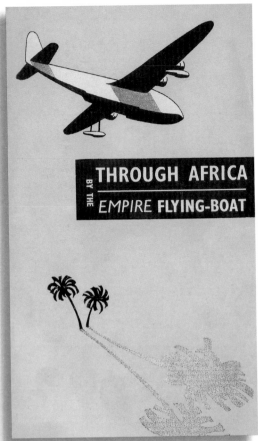

EAMS – Phase 1

Once the UK–Egyptian service was established, the EAMS expanded in three phases. The first opened the route to South Africa. The initial sector of the southbound route from Alexandria to Cairo lay across the delta of the Nile, a short 96-nautical-mile sector, alighting on the River Nile at Rod el Farag.

The next short sectors over the lower reaches of the Nile followed the course of the river to Juba, calling at Wadi Halfa, followed by an overland sector to Khartoum, bisected by the River Nile at the fourth cataract. Khartoum was the junction with the IAL service to Lagos via Fort Lamy. Night stops were made at the Grand Hotel. The hot, dry winds of the Khamsin, affected the northern sectors, occurring when low pressure approached the North African coast with a region of high pressure centred over Middle Egypt.

Between Khartoum and Lake Victoria, when either a strong southerly or a strong northerly wind was blowing at low level, 'boats could seek comparative calm at 7,500ft or 8,000ft.

From Juba, 'boats flying to Port Bell diverted, if conditions permitted, for a low pass over the Murchison Falls where the Victoria Nile thunders through a gorge 6m wide with spectacular results, on its way south to Lake Albert. Violent storms occurred during the rainy season on the sectors from the north of Khartoum to Juba and at any time between Juba and Lake Victoria.

Passengers crossing the equator for the first time, on the African service over Lake Victoria

LEFT Empire 'boats staging through East Africa, often had to dodge semi-submerged hippopotami on Lake Victoria, Uganda. *(Shutterstock)*

the neighbourhood in 1544. During the eighteenth century, pirates from Madagascar harried the settlers who were forced to withdraw. It was recolonised in the following century and since 1907 has superseded the old town of Mozambique as capital of Portuguese East Africa. The township is situated on the western shore of the Bay and has of recent years improved in appearance and conditions and is now ranked as one of the best health and pleasure resorts for up-country residents

JOHANNESBURG—LOURENÇO MARQUES—*Operated by South African Airways*
See map on page 24

This is a flight of nearly 300 miles. Leaving Johannesburg you head due east and before long pass over the railway which runs to the coast of Delagoa Bay, taking a more northerly route than ours. We then cross the Oliphant River—one of the tributaries of the Limpopo which has its mouth on the north shores of Delagoa Bay. The only place of any importance that we fly over is Carolina. In actual fact the town is growing rapidly—coal and asbestos are being worked in the neighbourhood and other minerals are known to exist. The main road to Swaziland starts from here. You may get a good view of the municipal dam from the air—it is reputed to afford excellent carp

26

and on the eastern route over the Lingga Archipelago south of Singapore, were given a certificate signed by the Commander of the aircraft to certify that they had crossed the Line.

The Port Bell alighting area was on Lake Victoria (height 3,717ft), the highest port on the route. Passengers left the aircraft and were taken by bus to Kampala for the night stop. The next sector was flown round the northern shore of the Lake to Kisumu.

The sector from Kisumu to the ocean at Mombasa was overland, climbing over the mountains of Kenya, some of which are over 10,000ft in height. Depending on weather conditions, Mount Kenya (17,058ft) was visible 65 nautical miles to port, and the twin snowcapped peaks of Mount Kilimanjaro (19,340ft), rising from its double wreath of white cloud, were to be seen some 38 nautical miles off the track to starboard, 150 nautical miles out from Mombasa. The flying boats called at Lake Navivasha, if inducement by way of passengers or freight offered and circumstances permitted, on southbound services only.

From Mombasa to the end of the line at Durban, the route was flown over the Indian Ocean. The 'boats could be night-stopped at the Hotel do Lumbo in Mozambique. The cyclone season for this part of the coast was from November to mid-May. Southwards from Mozambique to Durban, the route staged through optional refuelling stops at Beria, Inhambane, and Lourenco Marques. The alighting area in Durban was at Congella Airport on the substantially land-locked harbour of Durban. Total distance of this branch of the EAMS to Durban was 6,348 nautical miles. The sector distances are worth recording. Four were less than 200 nautical miles, five between 200 and 300, four between 300 and 400, and two between 300 and 400. When the Horseshoe Route was established after the collapse of France and the entry of Italy into the Second World War, Durban was to become the main base at the western end of the line.

EAMP – Phase 2

The second phase in February 1938, extended the EAMP to India, Burma and Malaya. From Alexandria, the eastern route turned north-eastwards across the eastern end of the Mediterranean Sea, crossing the coast of Palestine south of Haifa to drop down to a refuelling stop on Lake Tiberias, 689ft below sea level – the lowest point on the route. It then turned for a cross-country sector over the Syrian Desert to the Euphrates–Tigris basin, to alight on Lake Habbaniyah. The desert sectors were normally flown high to avoid turbulence from the heat. Sand and dust storms occurred from June to September, extending up to 12,000ft. Thunderstorms (in May and June and

ABOVE Passengers would have enjoyed views like this of shallow coastal waters and forests of the tropical coast of Mozambique. *(Shutterstock)*

FAR LEFT An inside page from the passenger guide booklet describing the route followed by the Empire 'boats on the northbound sector from Johannesburg, up the coast of Mozambique, to Lourenco Marques. *(British Airways Speedbird Heritage Centre)*

again in October and November) occurred up to 35,000ft. Both these storms could blot out all communication from ground to air.

From Lake Habbaniyah the route turned southwards down the river to Basra. This sector was subject to storms appearing instantly without any warning. The night stop was made at the Iraq Railway guesthouse at the combined land and marine airport on the west bank of the Shatt al-Arab, 2km north of the city of Basra. The Basra to Kuwait sector was the shortest on the route, a distance of 70 nautical miles. The normal route from Kuwait was direct to Dubai down the Persian Gulf, although some 'boats called at Bahrain on their way. Low-level flying over the Gulf was hot and bumpy.

The alighting area at Dubai was on a reach of the creek. The charge to IAL for alighting and an overnight stay was 5 rupees, with an additional 4 rupees for the night watchman. Passengers and crew were ferried ten miles from the creek in two Ford utilities, to sleep overnight at the combined Sharjah Fort and hotel, complete with its steel entrance door, loopholes for rifles, and encircling belt of barbed wire.

Departing from Dubai, the route lay eastwards across the desert, climbing to a safe height of 8,000ft to cross the mountain range. The sector from Dubai to Karachi direct was flown over the Gulf of Oman, following the southern coast of Persia. This part of the route was subject to monsoon conditions from June to August, with much turbulence and upward convection currents. Tropical storms were also frequent in May and June, and again in October and November. From the windows of the promenade cabin (flying eastbound) passengers could see some of the most extraordinary and fantastic rock formations of the Makran coastal range of mountains.

The third night stop was made at Karachi on Korangi Creek. Monsoons affected the route from Karachi to Singapore. Upper-air reports were available from most of the meteorological stations along the route, giving wind speeds and directions.

The dust storms that occurred over the Sind Desert were not of the same density as those over the Middle East, with visibility rarely dropping below 1,000m. Before and after the south-west monsoon, ground temperatures

could reach 46°C. Strong to very strong west and south-west winds increased in speed with height. Captains flying sectors across India often had two options. Either they could fly very low, sometimes between 200 and 300ft in the very hot and disturbed air, and risk upsetting the passengers, or they could climb higher into cooler and calmer air, to face head winds from 40 to 50kts. During the south-west monsoon, the route was covered in dense cloud with intervals of heavy rain. High ground was cloud-covered and wind direction and strength were difficult to forecast. Cumulus clouds over high ground, with their strong vertical air currents, could reach 15,000ft. Meteorological balloons could not be tracked through the overcast sky, so wind speed and direction had to be estimated from the synoptic chart, often incorrectly. Dead reckoning positions could not always be confirmed by radio D/F 'fixes' in heavy tropical storms, because of interference, making course-holding difficult, even on the comparatively short-sector distances. In these trying conditions, the higher the altitude the calmer the weather. Even in the worst of the south-west monsoon, the 'boats could be flying in sunshine above the clouds at 10,000 to 15,000ft. Accelerometers in the cabins recorded occasional bumps of 3g (2g bumps were common and 6g bumps were occasionally experienced in extreme monsoon conditions). In marginal conditions, the automatic pilot was often disconnected to allow both pilots to fly the aircraft manually together to secure a smoother ride for the passengers.

The sector from Karachi to Raj Samand was overland and often flown at between 500 and 1,000ft. An ancient reservoir complete with palace, temple, and dam was used as the alighting area. The water level here and at Gwalior varied considerably, and the 'boats had to radio ahead for alighting clearance. From Raj Samand the route continued overland to Gwalior to an alighting area on the lake of Madho Sagar to the west of the city.

Another overland sector brought the route to Allahabad. Because of headwinds, this sector was also often flown very low, 200 to 300ft, with accompanying turbulence from the

ground. The 'boats alighted at the confluence of the Jumna and Ganges rivers, where the river current was normally 7kts, but up to 14kts on occasions. The route continued overland to Calcutta.

The fourth night stop at Calcutta was made at the Great Eastern Hotel, considered by many experienced travellers to be the best hotel on the route. The alighting was made on the River Hooghly near the Howrah Bridge. The river was full of eddies and undercurrents, making taxiing difficult sometimes, and it was to claim *Centurion* on 12 June 1939 when, lightly loaded and carrying four passengers, it was involved in a freak accident while alighting on the river. The approach was made with full flap. The 'boat touched down near the Bally Bridge at about 90–95kts, and after running for some four or five seconds, the tail came up and *Centurion* slewed violently to port. The skin plating forward collapsed, causing the bow to dig into the water, and the aircraft started to sink. Captain Loraine, First Officer Murray, and Steward Carter were injured, and one of the passengers broke a leg. *Centurion* turned on its back and finally sank.

The route continued across the delta of the Ganges and the Sundarbans to cross the north

east of the Bay of Bengal. This part of the route was subject to tropical storms from April to November, and as the 'boats flew southwards they re-entered the monsoon area. Revolving storms, with torrential rain, developed over the Bay of Bengal at any season and the 'boats had to find their way around them. Akyab (an optional refuelling point), for example, could have as much as 250in of rain during the monsoons in May and June, with cumulo-nimbus cloud extending to 60,000ft.

The sector to Rangoon was flown down the west coast of Burma and thence across land and the Dawna mountain range to the alighting

ABOVE 'VE *Centurion* crashed on the River Hooghly at Calcutta on 12 June 1939. The hull broke in two as the aircraft turned over on its back. (*Author's collection*)

BELOW The Bally Bridge over the Hooghly in modern-day Kolkata (Calcutta). (*Wikimedia Commons*)

de Havilland DH86s that flew the spur service to Hong Kong.

The EAMP route turned almost due south over the Gulf of Siam to the island of Koh Samui. Continuing southwards, the route went down the 100° meridian, across the Malay peninsular to Penang. Depending on the service, the alighting was often at midnight, departing again at 03:00 to arrive at Singapore for breakfast at the Raffles Hotel and a night stop.

On the EAMP, the IAL crews 'slipped' at Singapore to take the next return westbound service from Australia. After July 1938, on some services the aircraft continued onwards with a QEA crew, while on others the eastbound service was flown in a QEA 'boat to Brisbane and Sydney.

EAMP – Phase 3

Finally, in the third phase in 1939, the Empire Air Mail Programme was completed to Australia and New Zealand. Departing Singapore to the south, the route lay over the Riau Islands and the Strait of Malacca to pick up the eastern coast of Sumatra, over the channel between the mainland and Banka Island, to turn southwards for a cautious approach to the heavily defended city of Batavia (Djakarta), hedged around with prohibited areas. The equator was crossed over the Lingga archipelago an hour out from Singapore, with certificates for first-time passengers. The Batavia to Sourabaya sector was flown along the north coast of Java for the seventh night stop at the Orange Hotel. From Sourabaya the route followed the north coasts of the islands of Bali and Lombok of the Dutch East Indies (Indonesia) to Bima on Sumbawa Island, to cross the Sumba Strait, skirting the northern coast of Sumba Island and then across the Savu Sea to Koepang.

The next 494 nautical-mile sector to Darwin was flown at 10,000ft to avoid the south-east prevailing winds in winter, to alight on the harbour with its tidal range of 24ft. The cyclone season was from December to March. British Power Boats built a special patrol and rescue launch (capable of 27kts at full throttle) for this sector, to be stationed at Darwin. The launch could rescue up to 50 persons unlucky enough

ABOVE Passengers were able to see the golden Shwe-Dagon Pagoda in Yangon (Rangoon) Myanmar from many miles away. *(Shutterstock)*

area 16km north of the city. The giant Shwe-Dagon Pagoda, covered with gold leaf, was clearly visible 16 nautical miles away and the 'boats often flew low over the pagoda to give the passengers a good view.

The Rangoon to Bangkok sector was partly across the Gulf of Martaban and then crossing the Burmese coast and over the border to Thailand, alighting on the River Menam at Bangkok. Bangkok was the base for the IAL

RIGHT Passengers could follow the progress of their journey on a fold-out map. *(British Airways Speedbird Heritage Centre)*

G-AE·UA

IMPERIAL AIRWAYS MAP CALCUTTA – SYDNEY

to ditch in the 'shark-infested' Timor Sea. The eighth night stop was spent at Darwin Cottage.

The first Australian sector of the route lay across the middle of Arnhem Land, crossing the coast of the Gulf of Carpentaria near Bickerton Island, to the base on Groote Eylandt on the hitherto uncharted Princess Elizabeth Bay with refuelling facilities that included a 140,000gal storage tank and a long submarine pipeline to the jetty. The next forward sector was over the Gulf of Carpentaria to the Queensland shoreline at Karumba. From Karumba the route was overland, crossing the northern part of Queensland and the Great Dividing Range to drop down to Townsville for the ninth night stop, alighting on the harbour. The route continued southwards along the Queensland coastline to Gladstone, flying over the Cumberland Islands and the Capricorn Channel, following the coastline to Brisbane to alight on the Pinkenbar Reach of the River Brisbane. The final sector of the route was southwards along the New South Wales coast to the terminus of the EAMP at Sydney, alighting at Rose Bay on the harbour, a total distance of 11,332 nautical miles. An analysis of sector distances from Southampton

ABOVE *Carpentaria* at the QANTAS Empire Airways maintenance base in Rose Bay, Sydney Harbour. *(British Airways Speedbird Heritage Centre)*

LEFT From Southampton to the crystal clear waters of Rose Bay and the EAMP flying boat terminal at Sydney, New South Wales, was a flying distance of 11,332nm (20,851km). *(Shutterstock)*

ABOVE **The New York terminal was at Port Washington on the eastern end of Long Island, alighting on Long Island Sound.** *(Shutterstock)*

ABOVE **Baggage label for Imperial Airways' Bermuda to New York service.** *(Author's collection)*

ABOVE **The New York terminal was at Port Washington on the eastern end of Long Island, alighting on Long Island Sound.** *(Shutterstock)*

BELOW *Clare* **at Port Washington, Long Island.**

BELOW RIGHT **Imperial Airways had specially designed their passenger seats, which were a source of much pride to the company.** *(British Airways Speedbird Heritage Centre)*

to Brisbane shows 14 to be between 200 and 300 nautical miles, 17 between 300 and 400, two between 400 and 500, one between 500 and 600, and one over 600 nautical miles.

A transatlantic mail service was also contemplated, and a potentially lucrative subsidiary service between Bermuda and New York was to be flown in pool with Pan American Airways. The New York terminal was at Port Washington on the east end of Long Island, alighting on Long Island Sound. This service was mostly for tourists rather than mail.

When IAL got their new Empire flying boats, they were more than satisfied with them, considering them to be the most successful marine aircraft ever produced. The 'boats were very popular with their crews and passengers. The passenger seats, which had been developed by IAL, were acknowledged to be the best and most comfortable available and the noise levels in the cabins were satisfactory. Passengers could move relatively freely about the cabins, although

too much movement could be felt on the control deck in the matter of tail trim.

There was one reservation – the matter of payload. A kilogram of payload was worth £27 per annum (c. £1,000 today). Payloads of the standard Mk I S.23 'boats varied, but were about 3,700kg. They could carry 1,500kg of mail and freight with 16 passengers or 750kg of mail and freight and 24 passengers, but could not lift 1,500kg of mail and freight, and 24 passengers. There was also an argument current as to whether passengers and mail would not be better completely separated and carried in different aircraft. The weight of trimming the passenger cabins of an Empire 'boat, including seats, bedding, an additional lavatory and the pantry equipment and stores, was between 900 and 1,000kg. The low passenger load factors on the EAMP meant that the comfortable appointments of the passenger accommodation and the provision of hotel-quality catering were not sold up to their full capacity.

World at war and the Horseshoe Route

On 9 April 1940, German armed forces invaded Denmark and Norway. Within the month both V3137 *Cabot* and V3138 *Caribou* had been destroyed by the Luftwaffe at the little Norwegian port of Bodø, while delivering radar equipment for the RAF – the first of several Empire 'boats destroyed during the war.

The German assault on the Low Countries began just over a month later on 10 May 1940. The eight-month stretch of the 'phoney' war was over. A weary, dispirited and ailing Mr Chamberlain resigned as Prime Minister, and Mr Churchill took his place. Soon the fighting had spread to northern France, involving the 'E' class aircraft in ferrying supplies to the RAF fighter squadrons in France, with the loss of one captain killed and one 'E' class aircraft set on fire. Yet, in spite of the fighting in France, the Empire services were maintained. On 30 May, for example, the brand new S.33 'boat *Cleopatra* departed Poole for India, but ten days later, the entry of Italy into the war brought the service to an end.

On the day that Italy entered the war (10 June 1940), *Clyde* and *Cathay* were westbound at Malta and Ajaccio, and *Caledonia* was eastbound at Corfu. All went on to complete their journeys. Sixteen 'boats were east or south of Alexandria. The IAL staff in Rome were granted diplomatic status and departed with the diplomats.

As Italy's move had been expected, planning was well advanced for setting up a service between Durban and Sydney. If the track of the service is traced on a Mercator projection map of the world it describes an inverted, rough-and-ready horseshoe; hence the name Horseshoe Route. The route was to be connected to the UK by a collection of ex-Imperial Airways Limited and ex-British Airways aircraft. The intended route lay across France, the western Mediterranean and the Sahara to Fort Lamy, and from there to join the Horseshoe Route at Khartoum. In the planning for the new service the collapse of French resistance had not been foreseen.

The Franco-German Armistice was signed on 22 June 1940, denying the over-flying of mainland France, and a week later the over-flying of French colonial territory was also banned, thus putting an end to the proposal to link the African operation to the United Kingdom across French territory.

Less than a fortnight after the Italian entry into the war, the first weekly Horseshoe Route services began from either end. The Poole–Lisbon flying boat service was in operation within the month, and the first West African service arrived at Lagos on 6 August 1940 via Lisbon, a 12-hour flight. Most of the service was over the ocean to Bathurst, giving Vichy-controlled Dakar a wide berth. The route continued to Freetown and Lagos. From Lagos, a direct ocean sector brought the service to Libraville and onwards to Leopoldville for an alighting on the River Congo. The Leopoldville–Coquilhatville sector followed the approximate

BELOW LEFT AND RIGHT The wreckage of Empire 'boats V3137 *Cabot* (left) and V3138 *Caribou* in the icy arctic waters at Bodø in Norway. *(Author's collection)*

ABOVE **G-AFCT,** *Champion*, **impressed into RAF service, on the slipway.** *(British Airways Speedbird Heritage Centre)*

line of the river. From Coquilhatville to Stanleyville, the route lay directly cross-country. The last sector of the West African service to join the Horseshoe Route was to Laropi (south of Juba), or Kisumu on Lake Victoria.

The start of the Horseshoe Route brought many changes to the interior accommodation

of the 'boats and to the cabin service. Many Horseshoe services were flown without a steward, with the flight clerk (or purser as he had by then become) standing in for him to dispense a much-reduced culinary service.

Champion and *Cathay* were used on a twice-weekly Poole-Lisbon shuttle service

RIGHT *Clare* **shows off her wartime camouflage colour scheme at Port Washington.**

to link up with the resumed Pan American Airways (PAA) service across the Atlantic to Lisbon. At the other end of the Horseshoe, the PAA transpacific service opened between San Francisco and Auckland, completing the link with the USA.

Clyde and *Clare*, in camouflage and with Certificates of Airworthiness allowing a take-off at 53,000lb, flew a series of five return transatlantic flights in August 1940, carrying mail and the first three westbound passengers across the Atlantic in a British aircraft. Atlantic ferry pilots made up the return load. The second service, departing 14 August, took the Under-Secretary of State for Air, Harold Balfour, across to the USA to sign the purchasing contract for BOAC's Boeing 314s. When the Atlantic season closed because of ice at Botwood, the two 'boats were switched to the West African service, to be joined by *Champion* early in 1941.

In September 1940, at the height of the Battle of Britain, the Horseshoe Route was reinforced by *Corinthian, Cassiopeia*, and *Cooee*, flown out from the UK via the West African route to join the Horseshoe Route at Lake Victoria. The 'boats had their Certificates of Airworthiness revised for the delivery flight for a take-off at 45,000lb. The three extra 'boats enabled the Horseshoe Route service frequency to be doubled to two flights per week.

One S.30 and two S.33 'boats were delivered in 1940, while two S.30s had been written off, leaving 23 standard S.23s, six S.30s, and two S.33s in service, the largest combined fleet in the history of the Empire flying boats.

With the route well established, it was political events that dominated the whole of the Horseshoe operations. The tide of war in Africa, the Mediterranean, and finally the Pacific, shifted back and forth. British forces pushed along the North African coast into Cyrenaica, with Benghazi being entered on 7 February 1941. At the same time, the operation to clear Italian

forces from Abyssinia and Italian Somaliland was proceeding. Addis Ababa was occupied on 4 April 1941 and soon after that the campaign was virtually over. In North Africa, the Italian army (reinforced by German armoured units of the Afrika Korps under the command of Field Marshal Rommel) pushed the depleted British army back to the Egyptian frontier. British troops had been withdrawn from the Desert Army and sent to Greece, in the forlorn hope of stemming the German invasion of Greece and Yugoslavia. By 20 April 1941, the German army was at Thermopylae, and in Athens a week later. The British and Greek forces were evacuated to Crete and North Africa from Kalamata, Nauplia, Rafina, and Monemvasia.

In April 1941, two of the Horseshoe 'boats, *Cambria* and *Coorong*, were detached for a three-week period to help evacuate Allied forces from Crete. Operating from Alexandria, they departed in the late afternoon to arrive at Souda Bay at last light for a 'night stop' and departed at next daybreak with RAF personnel. Flying boat crews were formed from a pool of five captains, five first officers, five radio officers, and three flight engineers. Once the crews were made up they were shuttled backwards and

ABOVE A 314 could dip a wing tip if the wind shifted unexpectedly, or if too tight a turn was attempted, so Boeing thoughtfully provided them with watertight wing tips. *(Boeing)*

forwards by car from Cairo to the 'boats at Alexandria.

The Crete sorties were flown at wave-top height, sometimes escorted by Sunderlands, sometimes the two 'boats flew together, and sometimes alone. Typical loads were 35 RAF men. No one worried about load sheets or load distribution. When the passenger hatch threshold was about to ship water, loading was halted. *Coorong* had the record with 47 passengers. The 13 round trips, the last on 5 May, carried a total of 469 passengers, most of whom had been previously rescued from Greece by Sunderlands. These extra flights, completed without mishap, were made without disturbance to regular Horseshoe services. Two weeks later, on 20 May 1941, the German airborne invasion of Crete (Operation Mercury) started at first light and was completed in some ten days.

In 1941, the 'boats on the Horseshoe Route had their passenger load increased to 30. Five passengers and the purser were in the forward cabin, seven passengers in the centre cabin (two on seats and five on a lower bunk), ten passengers in the promenade cabin (eight on seats and two on bunks), and eight in the aft cabin (six on seats and two on bunks). With this live load on board, the centre of gravity of the aircraft could be affected if there was any movement of passengers. So, once seated, passengers had to stay put.

The ultimately disastrous German attack on the Soviet Union (Operation Barbarossa) rolled across the border of a partitioned Poland on 22 June 1941. Syria was occupied by the Allies in the face of Vichy French resistance, and British and Russian troops took over Persia. In November, the first offensive by the Eighth Army opened, relieving Tobruk by the end of the year. In December, the Germans were fought to a standstill by the Red Army outside Moscow, and the Japanese brought themselves, and the United States of America, into the war.

The Horseshoe Route continued in operation through the year, flying the route from Durban to Sydney, but with increasing difficulty because of a shortage of aircraft and crews. Besides personnel, the 'boats were carrying mail to and from the UK, the majority for the Forces. Most of the mail was in the form of aerogrammes priced at threepence (3d) for the Services, sixpence (6d) for civilians, and a special rate of twopence (2d) for prisoners of war. The civilian rate was to remain fixed for 25 years.

Airgraphs were introduced into the Middle East when the first Kodak microfilm camera was flown out to Cairo. For the same price as an aerogramme a handwritten message was reduced to microfilm at the rate of 1,700 messages per 100ft of film, weighing 154g. Films were flown back to the UK where they were processed, folded, placed in window envelopes and passed to the GPO's London Postal Region for delivery. The originals were kept until the microfilms were safely in the UK. *Clare* was carrying 29 of these films when it disappeared over the Atlantic. The 50,000 Airgraphs on board were reprocessed and delivered within the fortnight. The first Airgraphs left Cairo on 21 April 1941, and the reciprocal service from the UK started in August 1941. By the time the service closed on 31 July 1945, some 350 million Airgraphs had been delivered.

The Mk I S.23 QEA 'boats in wartime service were stripped to the bone by removing the

cabin trimming, heating, and pantry – enabling them to carry an average of 31 passengers, with the take-off weight increased to 43,500lb.

For a period of about three weeks, the normal stops on the Horseshoe Route were disrupted at Lake Habbaniyah by an insurrection in Iraq. The RAF station on the shores of Lake Habbaniyah was attacked and the BOAC rest house looted. At the time the Mk I S.23 'boats were in the process of having their fuel system capacities modified from 652gal to 1,412gal. Those with increased tankage could overfly Iraq, so they ran a shuttle service between Cairo and Bahrain until the situation returned to normal. The former IAL base ship at Mirabella Bay in Crete (MV *Imperia*) was stationed in the Gulf of Aqaba in case it became necessary for the Horseshoe Route to be diverted eastwards to avoid Cairo. Aqaba was to be used for a short time as a refuelling stop.

Towards the end of the year, QEA crews took over the sectors from Singapore to Karachi to help the hard-pressed BOAC crews. To counter the expected entry of the Japanese into the Second World War, diversions from the eastern

end of the main Horseshoe Route, known as 'Phases', had been planned. Phase I omitted Bangkok as a night stop. Phase II diverted the route to omit Thailand, operating from Rangoon through Mergui and then to Singapore via Penang. Phase III omitted the Burma coast, from Rangoon to Port Blair in the Andaman Islands, to Sabang on Weh Island to the north of Sumatra and then, as Phase II, to Singapore via Penang. Phase IV omitted Malaya, operating down the west coast of Sumatra from Rangoon through Port Blair to Sabang, and Padang to Batavia, with refuelling stops at Sibolga and Benkulen. A shuttle service was to be run between Batavia and Singapore. The 'boats were switched to the reserve routes on 8 December 1941. From Auckland, the two TEAL 'boats were flying a series of 13 RF reconnaissance flights beside the flights across the Tasman to Sydney. One reconnaissance flight, RF3 on 21 August 1940 and flown by *Awarua*, lasted 12hr 58min.

The Poole–Foynes–Lisbon shuttle service was maintained by the three S.30 'boats, *Champion*, *Cathay*, and *Clare*. *Clyde* was

BELOW **Empire 'boat** ***Clare* of BOAC moored at Gibraltar after flying King George of Greece and Sir Stafford Cripps to the colony for a visit. On 12 October 1941,** ***Clare* made BOAC's first flight to Cairo, routed through Lisbon, Gibraltar and Malta. She was destroyed by fire off Bathurst, West Africa, on 14 September 1942.** *(Imperial War Museum CM6525)*

BELOW **Empire 'boat** ***Clare* of BOAC moored at Gibraltar after flying King George of Greece and Sir Stafford Cripps to the colony for a visit. On 12 October 1941,** ***Clare* made BOAC's first flight to Cairo, routed through Lisbon, Gibraltar and Malta. She was destroyed by fire off Bathurst, West Africa, on 14 September 1942.** *(Imperial War Museum CM6525)*

wrecked by a hurricane while at anchor on the River Tagus at Lisbon in February 1941. In the autumn of 1941, the military situation in the Mediterranean allowed a direct weekly Gibraltar to Cairo service to be operated by the West African 'boats, via Malta. The first Mediterranean sector was flown by *Clare* – a 9hr night flight, in complete radio silence, flying parallel to the Vichy-controlled coastline of North Africa. The 'boats turned at the Cape Bon lighthouse (fortunately still operating) to negotiate the 50 nautical-mile-wide corridor between Tunis and the fortified Italian island of Pantelleria. A turn eastwards brought them to an alighting at the RAF base on Malta, just before first light. The flare path had two lights, one on a wreck and the other on the control dinghy. A 9hr onward flight to Cairo, starting in the dark, completed the service. The return service often terminated on the calmer waters of the River Tagus at Lisbon rather than the more dangerous ocean swell off Gibraltar. The military situation in March 1942 brought this operation to a halt.

Clio and *Cordelia* were purchased by the Air Ministry from BOAC in July 1940 as replacements for the two S.30 'boats lost at Bodø in the Norwegian campaign. Converted to S.23M status, they were each equipped with two Boulton & Paul Type A four-gun power-operated turrets, one amidships on the starboard side, and the other in the tail. The fitting of the tail turret required considerable reshaping of the hull, the cropping of the rudder, and moving the trim tab. The aircraft were modified to carry six 430lb internally stowed depth charges. Limited armour plating and ASV radar completed the conversion, and they emerged in March 1941 as S.23Ms with RAF serials AX659 and AX660. The 'boats were delivered to 119 Squadron RAF at Bowmore off the west coast of Scotland for convoy protection and transport. AX659 *Clio* flew its first convoy protection patrol (Convoy OG0.60) on 27 April for 8hr 14min. Its brief service of five months with the RAF ended when the aircraft crashed on a test flight near Bowmore, the unlucky 13th Empire 'boat to be written off. AX659 *Clio* required the starboard outer engine to be changed, which was carried out on the water. On the test flight the replacement engine failed. Then the starboard inner engine stopped

because of contaminated fuel, leaving no power on the starboard wing. With the aircraft flying on the two port side engines, flying speed was lost during the turn, the 'boat stalled and crashed. No 119 Squadron RAF was disbanded, and AX660 *Cordelia* spent six weeks with No 413 (RCAF) Squadron before being sold back to BOAC to be converted again to a standard wartime S.23.

Before the year was out, British troops on the Malayan peninsula were at the second degree of readiness, awaiting the Japanese invasion. On 26 November 1941, the Japanese First Air Fleet embarked on six aircraft carriers with escorts and sailed eastwards towards the Hawaiian Islands. By dawn on 7 December 1941, the carrier group was 200 nautical miles north of Oahu. At 07:55 the attack on Pearl Harbour began. Japan had entered the war. At the same time, other Japanese aircraft were attacking RAF airfields in Malaya as convoys of Japanese ships landed their troops along the eastern beaches.

Singapore and Penang were also bombed. By the end of December, the situation was so dangerous that all flying boat operations south of Rangoon were suspended. *Castor* was at Rangoon, eastbound, and *Ceres* at Mergui, westbound. Phase III, the reserve route from Rangoon to Singapore via Port Blair, Sabang and Penang, came into operation immediately. On 29 December *Cassiopeia* crashed on take-off at Sabang, after refuelling there for the first time. Spare engines, some stores, and personnel were moved from Singapore to Batavia on 13 February 1942, two days before the surrender of Singapore Island.

Two S.23s and one S.30 were written off during 1941, leaving twenty-one S.23s, five S.30s and two S.33s in service.

In the Western Desert, the British Eighth Army was fighting a series of rearguard actions along the coast of Cyrenaica until the end of June 1942, when it took up a defensive position at El Alamein some 110 nautical miles from Cairo and the Horseshoe Route. MV *Imperia* was still at its station in the Gulf of Aqaba in case it became necessary for the Horseshoe Route to be diverted eastwards should German and Italian forces break through. The military situation in the desert remained virtually static while a reinforced Eighth Army was made ready for the Battle of El Alamein in October 1942. The retreat of the German and Italian forces from El Alamein started on 2 November 1942 and the threat to the Horseshoe Route, from this quarter at least, was removed for ever.

The year 1942 was a disastrous one for the Empire 'boats. Operations by the Japanese forces dominated the situation at the eastern end of the route. The Japanese invasion of the Malayan peninsula ended with the surrender of Singapore on 15 February 1942, and the Horseshoe was broken, with the service turned round at Calcutta. The last service out of Singapore, in darkness without a flare path, lifted 43 women and children in either *Camilla* or *Corinna*. The flight was mentioned on Tokyo radio the same afternoon. The Horseshoe was to remain broken for three and three-quarter years until *Coriolanus* flew in to Singapore on 8 October 1945 to evacuate returned prisoners of war.

By the end of the month, a series of Japanese landings were made on either side of the erstwhile Horseshoe Route. The Japanese Western Force invaded Sumatra and Java. Units of the Japanese Central Force landed on southern Borneo, Celebes, Timor, Bali and the eastern end of Java. The defenders were overwhelmed, and by 8 March 1942 the whole of the Dutch East Indies was in Japanese hands.

In 1942, 15 'boats were in British registration and working on the Horseshoe or West African routes, 11 were either on charter to the RAAF or in QEA ownership, and two belonged to TEAL. The Empire 'boats isolated in Australia to the east of the break in the Horseshoe Route were in the thick of the action. The nine aircraft destroyed or written off during the year left a total of 19 in operation. *Corio* was shot down by Japanese fighters on 29 January. A month later, on 27 February, A18-12 *Coogee* was lost after a mishandled alighting at Townsville. The next day *Circe* (Captain W.B. Purton, First Officer M.W. Bateman, Radio Officer H.G.A. Oates, Pursers L.J. Hogan and W.R. Bartley and 16 passengers, including the Netherlands Consul General, his wife, and daughter) was lost without trace about 160 nautical miles out from Tjilatjap on the last of the shuttle services to Broome. *Coriolanus*, flying a few minutes ahead, heard *Circe* give a last position report

at 10:25. Nothing else was heard, so the 'boat was presumably shot down by Japanese fighters. A search by *Corinna* found no trace.

Within the week two more 'boats, A18-10 *Centaurus* and *Corinna*, were caught on the water at Broome and destroyed. On the water in the harbour and roadsteads were, besides A18-10 *Centaurus*, two US Navy Consolidated Catalinas, four Dutch Marine Luchvaart Dienst Catalinas, two RAF Catalinas, and five Dutch licence-built Dornier Do24s. Most of the Dutch 'boats had flown in from Java to refuel before departing to safer destinations, loaded with some 100 women and children of the families of the crews. Before dispersal could be arranged, the anticipated raid took place. At 09:20, nine Japanese Zero A6M2 fighters from the 23rd Air Flotilla swept in over the town. Three Zeros circled above keeping top cover while the remaining six, in line astern, shot up the flying boats at anchor. A18-10 *Centaurus* was the first to be attacked with incendiary bullets. The RAAF crew managed to get the inflatable life raft over the side and escape before the aircraft caught fire, making their way towards the shore picking up survivors from the Dutch 'boats as they went, finally packing 13 people into their five-man raft. *Corinna*, in the process of refuelling from the lighter *Nichol Bay*, was the next 'boat to be attacked. The lighter's master, Captain Mathison, cast off immediately and, although loaded with 180 drums of aviation spirit, began searching for survivors in the water. The QEA crew on *Corinna* jumped for their lives before the aircraft went up in flames. Finding a

dinghy floating nearby, they joined in the search for survivors. The Japanese pilots made no attempt to strafe survivors in the water or the group of passengers on the jetty. Beside some rifle fire, the only effective defence against the attack came from a single machine gun, which had been taken out of one of the Dutch 'boats and was ashore being checked for a fault. Using his forearm as a rest, the gunner fired at the attacking Zeros and succeeded in bringing one of them down. A18-10 *Centaurus* was the 18th, and *Corinna* the 19th Empire 'boat to be written off. In 2001, archaeologists from the Western Australian Maritime Museum searched Broome Harbour with side scan sonar, discovering many underwater wrecks, two of which are believed to be the Empire 'boats.

Two weeks later *Corinthian* crashed while alighting on Darwin Harbour, bringing the total number of aircraft destroyed in the first three months of the year to six. Leading an apparently charmed existence *Camilla*, at its mooring in Darwin Harbour, rode out the Japanese air raid unharmed except for a few minor perforations. The other casualties were A18-11 *Calypso,* a rescue attempt that went wrong off Daru, New Guinea on 9 August, and *Clare*, destroyed by fire in the air over the Atlantic between Bathurst and Lisbon on 14 September.

Clare had departed Lagos at daybreak for Bathurst, refuelling at Freetown. At Bathurst a new crew (Captain Musson, First Officer A.D.C. Jenkins, Second Officer A.O. Cundy, and Radio Officers E.F.G. Brent and J.A. Wytcherley) took over for the sector to Lisbon. Captain Musson preferred to fly tangents to a 60 nautical-mile circle to edge his way round the Vichy French city of Dakar rather than the more customary 20 nautical-mile radius. One hour out of Bathurst the captain decided to return, having lost an engine. Minutes later a request for 'Flares' was followed by 'SOS Fire'. *Clare* crashed in the dark some 30 minutes' flying time from Bathurst. The next day all available aircraft searched without success. On 16 September a BOAC Catalina (Captain J.C. Parker, Second Officer Talbot and Navigator D. McGregor) searched to the west of the assumed track. McGregor had flown with Captain Musson before and knew of his preference of giving Dakar a wide berth. They found six bodies and wreckage. *Ceres* was written off after a fire in the maintenance hangar at Durban on 1 December.

Passenger loads of 40 or more were flown by the 'boats in RAAF service, mostly on evacuation flights. A18-11 *Calypso* (Flt Lt M. Mather) and A18-12 *Coogee* (Flt Lt L. Grey) between them rescued 86 RAAF personnel from boats at a rendezvous on the open sea, 35 nautical miles south of Rabaul. The (unconfirmed) record passenger load is believed to have been 60 women, children, and wounded evacuated from Ambon to Darwin by an RAAF 'boat.

Eight S.23s and one S.30 were lost during 1942, leaving thirteen S.23s, four S.30s and two S.33s in service. Of the nineteen 'C' and 'A' flying boats remaining in service at the beginning of 1943, thirteen were engaged on the Horseshoe and African routes, four in Australia, two on charter to the RAAF and two under the control of the Australian government, and the two TEAL 'boats on the Auckland–Sydney service. The figures for the Horseshoe Route for the year ending March 1943, with two months estimated, show that the services from Durban to Calcutta, the UK to West Africa and Lagos and Port Bell were operating with a 91% passenger load factor.

The war in the Pacific had moved from Papua to New Guinea in a series of actions along the north coast. The United States Fifth Air Force had gained superiority in the air, and in September 1943 both Salamaua and Lae had been captured. The two Empire 'boats on charter with the RAAF continued to serve with 41 Squadron RAAF, delivering personnel and stores to Port Moresby and the newly captured Merauke. Both aircraft were handed back to QEA in the middle of the year, so ending their wartime service. The return of *Coolangatta* and *Clifton* brought QEA's Empire 'boat fleet back to three aircraft.

At the end of 1943 the Empire 'boat fleet total stood at 18 (12 S.23s, 4 S.30s, and two S.33s). One 'boat was lost during the year, *Camilla* (Captain A.A. Koch), off Port Moresby after battling a storm for more than six hours. Thirteen 'boats were flying on the Horseshoe and spur services, three were flying with QEA on charter to the Australian government, and the two TEAL 'boats were engaged on the trans-Tasman service.

Two of QEA's 'boats, *Coolangatta* and *Clifton*, were lost during 1944, both by alighting accidents and both in Sydney Harbour. *Clifton* was the 26th and last of the original 42 'boats to be written off.

From 1940 onwards the 'boats had maintained the Horseshoe Route until it finally closed on 12 March 1947 when *Caledonia* departed Durban for Southampton after 6 years, 37 weeks and about 5 days, more than twice as long as the EAMP.

In February 1945, the postal arrangements were revised to give a 1d per ounce outbound mail service from the UK. For the Armed Services, mail to the UK was carried without charge. This service undercut the aerogramme and Airgraph services, both of which closed by the end of the year. The war in Europe came to an end on 29 April 1945 when German envoys signed the terms of unconditional surrender, and all hostilities in Europe ceased on 7 May. By the end of the month, BOAC and QANTAS had instituted a joint weekly service from Hurn to Sydney, using Avro Lancastrian aircraft.

The Japanese domination of China, Burma, Borneo and the Philippine Islands was ending, and the war was brought to Japan. Boeing B-29 bombers of the XXI Bomber Command, US 20th AF, based in the Mariana Islands, started a systematic bombing campaign to paralyse Japanese industry and bring city life to a standstill. The incendiary bomb raids were halted to assess the effect of the first, and then the second, atomic bomb. Ten days later, on 19 August 1945, Japanese envoys arrived on the island of Ie Shima near Okinawa to arrange an unconditional surrender. The surrender documents were signed, under the watchful eye of General MacArthur, on the deck of the battleship USS *Missouri* anchored in Tokyo Bay on 2 September. After six years and a day, the Second World War was at an end.

The Horseshoe Route continued with the surviving aircraft suffering an increasing number of minor accidents and incidents. The Johannesburg (Vaaldam) to Durban spur service ended with the 151st flight. The trans-Tasman route continued and QEA opened a service to Suva. At the end of September 1945, John Lankester Parker took Sunderland V, TX293, off the Medway at Rochester on a test flight for the last time as Chief Test Pilot of Short Bros, ending a remarkable career spanning 29 years.

The fleet composition at the end of 1945 was unchanged, and for the first year since 1936, no 'boats were written off during the year.

A BOAC memo stated that flying boats would continue in service for 'two or three years' until landplanes could meet the demand. It was also suggested that some flying boats should be kept in service for possible new routes and to enable the techniques of flying and handling to be kept alive. BOAC ceased to use the facilities at Foynes in April 1946, and a month later opened a service to Sydney, in cooperation with QANTAS, using Short Hythe flying boats. In June, PAA flew the first direct transatlantic service flight from New York to London Heathrow.

Decline of the Empires

On 17 October 1946, *Canopus* arrived back in the United Kingdom for the last time. A week and a day later it was handed over for scrapping at Hythe, after a service life of ten years with 15,026 hours on the log. The first was followed by the last. By the end of the month, the last of the Empire 'boats to be launched, *Cleopatra* (10,513 hours), had arrived back and was scrapped.

The Empire 'boats scrapped at Hythe were beached, hauled out, and their engines and reusable equipment removed. The spars were cut with oxyacetylene torches and the hulls hacked to pieces with axes as they stood on their beaching chassis. The 'produce' was trimmed to a convenient size to fit into a 3-ton lorry to be taken to the melting-down furnaces. The residual value of an Empire 'boat for scrap is not known. The produce of the meltdown furnaces had many uses. Some was used to make crankcase covers for cars, and some of the metal found its way into domestic kitchenware. A small amount of the meltdown was cast into commemorative ashtrays, weighing 300g each. The words 'BOAC IMPERIAL AIRWAYS SHORT C CLASS 1936–1946' and the Speedbird logo were moulded inside. The registration plate and logbooks of *Coriolanus* are in the QANTAS Museum at Longreach, Queensland.

On 12 June 1946 an announcement was made in Parliament that the Seaplane Works and the Rochester Airport factory would have to close, as both were considered to be inadequate for the needs of the day. The last aircraft launched down the slipway at Rochester was G-AHIL, an S.45 Solent Mk 3 (Construction number S.1300) on 8 April 1948. The Seaplane Works at Rochester were finally closed in July 1948. It was almost 30 years since N.4000, the first Short-built flying boat, was lifted by crane into the Medway – the slipway not then being ready.

The Works have almost entirely disappeared beneath flats and houses. Nothing has been left behind that would be recognisable to anyone who knew the Works in 1940. Even the slipway has now disappeared. A plaque at the entrance to the former Seaplane Works records their location. The Wickham Reach of the River Medway was bridged in 1963 to the west of the Works by an elegant prestressed concrete structure by Freeman, Fox & Partners to carry the M2 motorway.

Echoes of the Empires

No complete 'boat has survived. Rather than being scrapped, *Cathay* was offered to the Science Museum in London, for preservation as part of the National Aeronautical Collection, but regretfully the offer had to be declined. The museum had suffered the loss of about one-third of its display accommodation through bombing during the Second World War and had no space available to house the proffered 'boat. Fragments of cylinder and the data plate of one of the engines of V3138 *Caribou*, rescued by divers from the wreckage on the seabed, are in the Luftfahrtshistoriske Museum at Bodø, Norway, together with a compass housing, an airscrew boss, and part of one of the blades.

Some ephemera exist. At least one of the Frog 1:72 scale acetate plastic models is known to be still intact. Frog quaintly described the 'boats as if they were surface vessels as 'quadruple-screwed monoplane boat seaplanes with a gross register of 18.375 tons' with the 'quadruple Pegasus machinery' quoted in shaft horse-power. Model kit 21P for the 'Short "Empire" ocean-going liner' was on sale between 1938 and 1941 at a cost of 15 shillings. The acetate material from which the model parts were moulded was not particularly stable, so any surviving models could by now have twisted out of shape, despite the plywood mainplane spar and transverse bulkhead ('spar frame') that Frog provided as part of the kit. The individual steel moulding dies for the models survived until 1946, but they were scrapped when the 'boats were. Dinky Toys produced their own version of the Empire 'boat as a small diecast model (No 60r), priced at one shilling. These models are now collectors' items worth between £100 and £300. One of them, registered as G-ADHM *Caledonia*, is

LEFT Like her sister 'boats, Tasman Empire Airways' ZK-AMA, *Aeotearoa*, met an undignified end. *(Author's collection)*

in its original box in a showcase in the Solent Sky Museum at Southampton, together with other memorabilia of the 'boats and their connection with Southampton Water. Nearby in the museum is a beautifully made model of 'UY *Capella* undergoing a daily check on the port inner engine. One of the full-colour posters, originally published in 1936, has been republished. Unaware of future problems with the mounting of the bunks in the air, it shows three passengers, either in their bunks or about to go to retire.

The National Film Archive holds two of the three IAL promotional films as part of their collection. The films were made circa 1937 by the Strand Film Company for IAL on 35mm highly flammable, and increasingly fragile, acetate stock with soundtrack. The titles, 'Watch and ward in the air', 'Air outpost', and 'The future is in the air' were made under the supervision of Paul Rotha and directed by Alexander Shaw and Ralph Keene. The music was composed by William Alwyn and Raymond Bennell. The commentaries were written by Graham Greene and spoken by Stuart Legg and Ivan Scott. 'Watch and ward in the air' was issued by the British Airways Archive Collection in a VHS format video. A portrait bust of Oswald Short was made by sculptor Charles Dyson-Smith. Its whereabouts is unknown.

The remains of at least ten 'boats lie under the water around the world, and with them some of their crews and passengers. *Cavalier* lies in the deep water of the Atlantic at N 37° 17' and W 69° 45'. Divers report that parts of V3137 *Cabot* are still on the seabed in

fairly shallow water off the Island of Mauren to the north of Bodø, inside the Arctic Circle. *Cassiopeia*, its hull broken in two pieces, is just outside the entrance to Sabang Harbour. The bodies of one of the passengers and the baby were never found. *Corio*, on a flight from Darwin to Sourabaya to evacuate women and children, was shot down off the mouth of the River Noelmini, near Koepang. Three crew and 15 passengers did not survive. *Circe*, complete with its crew of four and 30 passengers, is somewhere in the deep water between Tijlatjap and Broome, believed to have been shot down by Japanese fighters while on the last of the shuttle flights on 28 February 1942. The final message ever received was a position report at 10:25, about 130 nautical miles out from Tijlatjap. *Corinthian* is believed to be still in Darwin Harbour, although its whereabouts are not known, after breaking up and sinking during a normal alighting on the night of 21/22 March 1942, in good weather. Captain Ambrose was seriously injured, two passengers were killed, and two seriously injured. The shattered remains of A18-10 *Centaurus* and *Corinna* lie under the water off Broome, Western Australia. An underwater side scan sonar survey of the harbour by archaeologists from the Western Australian Maritime Museum in 2001 revealed evidence of the wrecks. One of two Empire 'boats is at S 18° 00' 48" and E 122° 15' 12", and anecdotal evidence indicates that it is probably A18-10. Underwater photographs show what seems to be an engine, and also evident are the cooling gills and the blade of an airscrew.

Chapter Four

Salvaging *Corsair*

Long-haul air travel in the thirties was a luxurious adventure for passengers, although for the airline flying the routes it was often anything but routine. When Empire 'boat *Corsair* force-landed on a river in the cheerless interior of the Belgian Congo, her sojourn turned into a long, drawn-out – but ultimately successful – salvage operation.

OPPOSITE African equatorial savannah in southern Sudan, close to where the Imperial Airways Empire 'boat *Corsair* landed on the River Dangu in the Belgian Congo in 1939. This photograph, taken in the rainy season, shows a river winding its way across the landscape. *(Shutterstock)*

The tiny African village of Faradje takes a lot of finding on the map. Lying only 3 degrees north of the Equator, in the Belgian Congo, it was here, on 14 March 1939, that the Imperial Airways Empire 'boat *Corsair* was forced to alight after straying off course while flying home to England from South Africa.

Commanded by Captain E.S. Alcock (brother of the famous John Alcock who had made the world's first successful transatlantic crossing by an aircraft), with a crew of First Officer W.L. Garner, Radio Officer G.W. Cussans, Flight Clerk Parsons and Steward Riddock, *Corsair* had staged through Port Bell, Lake Victoria, from where she took off at 06:15 on 14 March, with mail and passengers, heading north for Juba on the banks of the White Nile in Sudan. At 10:00, she made a forced alighting on the River Dangu in the north-eastern corner of the Belgian Congo, about 130nm south-west of Juba.

Bad luck in alighting

Captain E.S. Alcock alighted on the Dangu in a masterly piece of flying – the waterway was only about 50yd wide, little more than the wingspan of the Empire 'boat. It could have been a happy landing had it not been for a submerged rock which, towards the end of the run, tore a large piece out of the chine and damaged the port wing float. Reacting quickly,

ABOVE *Corsair* seen in better days, riding at anchor on the Sea of Galilee at Tiberias. *(US Library of Congress)*

RIGHT After a forced landing on the River Dangu, *Corsair* slowly slipped back into the water. *(British Airways Speedbird Heritage Centre/Mike Cussans collection)*

Alcock opened the throttles and ran *Corsair* towards the steep riverbank where here he held her by her engines until all passengers had been disembarked, thankfully without injury. Then she slid gently back into the shallow water and sank, although luckily not deeply enough to drown the engines, except for one carburettor.

Corsair was searched for and found by the Empire 'boat *Clio* and an RAF Wellesley. The passengers and crew had been rescued by the Belgian Resident Officer and driven to Aba, from where the passengers, salvaged mail and baggage were picked up by Empire 'boat *Centurion* (Captain F.V.W. Foy).

This forced alighting on the Dangu was the start of a monumental salvage operation involving recovery teams from Short Brothers and Imperial Airways. If the engineering challenges were not enough in themselves, the recovery team also faced epic struggles with the river, heat, disease and other, often appalling, difficulties.

Damage assessment and repairs

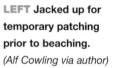

A repair party from Short Brothers and Imperial Airways was dispatched to the Dangu to work on *Corsair*. They estimated the time to rebuild the damaged hull to be six weeks, although the actual time proved to be nearer 15 weeks.

First they had to strip her of as much weight as possible, including removing her four engines and cabin furnishings, thereby allowing her to be jacked under one wing from the bank and raised on the other side by a raft of oil drums. This was achieved by filling oil drums with water, partially submerging them and then pumping them out, lifting the boat. With the hole now above water level, a temporary tarpaulin patch was put on and *Corsair* beached with the aid of a beaching chassis, specially transported there, and the muscle of some 200 or 300 native convicts. Once on the bank a more permanent repair was made and the engines reinstalled.

The damage to *Corsair* was substantial: there were tears to Frames 12 to 24, extensive damage to the keel, stringers and floor supports, the plating of the port side planing bottom, and the forward and rear main spar

ABOVE All four engines and propellers were removed to lighten Corsair ready for lifting. *(Alf Cowling via author)*

LEFT Note the beaching chassis underneath the hull. *(Alf Cowling via author)*

LEFT Jacked up for temporary patching prior to beaching. *(Alf Cowling via author)*

BELOW Repairing damage to the hull. *(Alf Cowling via author)*

frames (Frames 15/16 and 20/21) were damaged below the centre cabin.

In England, with full workshop facilities it would have been a relatively straightforward job to effect the necessary repairs, but these had to be carried out on a riverbank in equatorial Africa. The engineers had no heat-treating furnaces and no power riveters to hand, and the only roof over their heads was the wing of the aircraft. Each night they slept at Aba, a small village of some 30 to 40 Europeans, which was a 40-mile drive away.

While repairs were under way it was decided that the river needed to be made good enough for a flying boat to take off. A stone barrage was built to bank up the water using native prisoner labour supplied by the Belgian Congo authorities, a road was cut through 2,000yd of bush to link up with the nearest road, and stone quarries were opened on each bank of the river. Then wooden box frames, made from local timber, were placed across the stream at 10ft intervals to form the barrage and were filled with stone transported by the natives. 'Antbed', an unusual sort of earth material from which anthills are made in the tropics, was used to make the barrage watertight. A mat of rushes and canes was also woven along one face of the barrage to guard against further leaks.

TOP AND ABOVE Building the barrage. A dam was constructed to raise the water level. Note the mat of rushes and the box frames to be filled with stone. *(Alf Cowling via author)*

RIGHT The rains came, inundating the flood plain of the Dungu and hampering the salvage effort. *(British Airways Speedbird Heritage Centre)*

Going home again – nearly

By 13 July all was ready and *Corsair* was prepared for the take-off early the next morning. As a precaution, as many rocks as possible had been blasted from the stream but the conditions were far from ideal as the water level was low. Markers were strung across the river, between which the 'boat had to pass to avoid the rock. With Captain Alcock at the controls, assisted by First Officer Garner, the engines were opened up to full power for take-off. The port side engines responded but those on the starboard side failed to react.

The 'boat started its take-off run but as it gathered way the nose came up so far that Captain Alcock could not see the markers. The starboard wing float hit the water and *Corsair* swung out of control, colliding with a submerged rock on the right-hand side of the river. She came to rest on the rock and then slipped off back into the water, there to remain for two months.

Corsair had been holed once more, this time above and below the waterline – it had a 10ft tear in the starboard planing bottom between Frames 10 and 14, with water flooding into Nos 1, 2 and 3 bilges. The aircraft was pumped out and the hole patched, the patching being done half in and half out of the water. It was beached and the damaged plates drilled off and replaced. The repair was completed with the fitting of the planing bottom and side plates and the chine angle replaced.

ABOVE The aftermath of the abortive first attempt to take off. The large rock in the river between the aircraft and the bank was hit by Captain Alcock on his take-off run and was duly christened 'Alcock's rock'. *(Alf Cowling via author)*

LEFT Oil drum flotation tanks were used to raise *Corsair* after sinking for the second time. *(Alf Cowling via author)*

LEFT Stuck in the mud as the river began to dry up. *(Alf Cowling via author)*

ABOVE Imperial Airways salvage team outside their makeshift 'mess' on the riverbank. Despite their awful living conditions, they could still manage a laugh as the humorous sign for the 'Dungu Aircraft Coy' shows. From left to right: Radio Operator Wytcherley, Roy Sisson, Love, Ernie Carroll (standing) and Alf Cowling. Standing back left is the team's *askari*, who wears a suit made from *Corsair*'s seat upholstery. *(Alf Cowling via author)*

LEFT It took a week to get it high and dry out of the water again. *(Alf Cowling via author)*

LEFT Imperial Airways engineers beside *Corsair*. *(British Airways Speedbird Heritage Centre/Mike Cussans collection)*

OPPOSITE PAGE Engines are checked and run-up. *(Alf Cowling via author)*

They try again

With the wet season now over, the river level was falling and salvage was thought to be impossible. Dismantling was about to begin when in September an Imperial Airways survey team arrived from Alexandria headed by George 'Jock' Halliday. They decided that salvage was still possible and asked for another attempt to be made.

This time a more elaborate barrage was built. Trees were cut down and the five engineers went through the whole disheartening business of refloating and repairing the boat once again. The barrage, which was 10ft high, backed the water up to 4ft 0in, and gave 5ft of water over the highest rock. The boat drew 3ft 6in at its take-off weight of 30,162lb, at which weight her commander, Captain J.C. Kelly-Rogers, was confident he could fly her off. While the repairs were in progress, a series of trials involving Captains Bailey and Alcock were made to get a 'boat with a similar load off Southampton Water to assess the probability of success on the Dangu. It was found that the 'boat should get off in 375yd at Faraje.

Take-off at last

A length of 600yd had been made available for take-off on the Dangu. When it was remarked to Captain Kelly-Rogers how lucky he was to get as much as 600yd of such a river straight, he replied, 'It wasn't.' To assist in steering the take-off on the 50yd-wide river, wicker baskets were made and placed at intervals along the bank as sighting marks for Rogers.

In the cool of the early morning of 6 January 1940, *Corsair* was lifted out of the Congo under her own power. With a crew of four, one of whom was positioned at the stern of the 'boat

with the anchor in case of trouble, she took off downstream quite comfortably, and Kelly-Rogers held her down to give a little more flying speed before eventually climbing away. Soon they were at Juba for a refuelling stop, and then flew a normal transit to Alexandria where *Corsair* underwent a full maintenance check during a three-day stay before returning home. It was found that a wrongly wired wireless receiver or faulty reversing switch were possible factors behind the forced alighting on the Dangu.

On 15 January, Kelly-Rogers landed *Corsair* in England, having spent some ten months lying on – and in – a small river in the heart of Africa.

ABOVE most of the salvage team had left for home before *Corsair's* second and ultimately successful attempt to fly off the Dangu. Alf Cowling is second from left.
(Alf Cowling via author)

BELOW **Ready to go.** *(Alf Cowling via author)*

BELOW Jack Kelly-Rogers joined Imperial Airways in 1935 and his airmanship, experience and leadership qualities were often called upon for the more hazardous and prestigious assignments. In 1937 he flew the first Empire 'boat service along the Nile to Kisumu on Lake Victoria, and was in regular rotation as a captain on the lengthy Egypt–India–Australia route. In 1939 he flew Imperial's first transatlantic service to Canada and the United States. Most famously, in 1940, Kelly-Rogers rescued *Corsair* from the River Dangu in the Belgian Congo.

Chapter Five

Anatomy of the 'C' class

To make the best use of internal space, Arthur Gouge's design for a deep, narrow hull allowed for Empire passengers and flight crew to be accommodated on two decks. Innovative construction techniques were used in the wings and hull of the four-engined cantilever monoplane 'boats, which also benefitted from the widespread use of light-alloys in their manufacture.

OPPOSITE Shorts S.26, G-AFCJ, *Golden Fleece,* under construction at Rochester. *(Shorts)*

RIGHT A general view across No 3 Shop. The first hull is centre background, with the second hull emerging from its gantry (right). The starboard mainplane in the foreground is a standard wing to be fitted to the first hull. In the far left background is the aft end of one of the Singapore 'boats going through No 3 Shop at the same time. *(Shorts)*

The design for the Mk I S.23 'boat had been submitted to IAL at the end of June 1934, an 'instruction to proceed' was received on 24 January 1935 and a confirming order placed on 19 February for two aircraft, a 'prototype' and a 'Bermuda' 'boat, for delivery on 1 May and 1 June 1936 respectively, with a proviso that a further ten aircraft could be ordered not later than 31 May. During the construction of the 'prototype'

time had slipped somewhat. It was launched two months after it should have been delivered.

Despite a search in all the obvious places, no production drawings or prints have been found except for a print issued by the Jig and Tool Drawing Office showing the shop truck used in No 3 Erecting Shop. The truck was inserted beneath a completed hull so that it could be withdrawn from the gantry.

Hull

The Empire 'boats were designed to operate from the waters of sheltered harbours. The hull had to conform to the requirements of Air Publication (AP) AP 1208, the Airworthiness Handbook for Civil Aircraft requiring the minimum hull volume to be 4.5 times greater than the volume of the maximum displacement. The volume of an Empire hull was 9,800cu ft, or about 2.5 times that required by AP 1208. The block coefficient was 0.675.

The maximum beam dimension of all Empire 'boats was 10ft. One of Arthur Gouge's major objectives for the new hull was a significant decrease in the beam. Narrower hulls meant less aerodynamic drag and lower structural weight.

Once the design drawings had been completed, the lines of the hull were laid out, shipbuilding fashion, full size on the Mould Loft floor to be checked for truth and any necessary corrections made to the drawings. Production started in the Drawing Office, stretched out along the back of the Seaplane Works, above

BELOW The hull of the first Empire 'boat – minus the coupé, but mated with the tail aft of Frame 42 – newly withdrawn from the gantry, perched on the shop truck. The hull has been turned on to the centre line of the main doors of No 3 Shop with the nose pointing towards the main doors, ready for eventual roll-out. The date is 8 February 1936 and the time, 16:15. The starboard half mainplane is evident to the right of the photo, beneath the tail. *(Shorts)*

and behind Nos 11 and 13 Shops. The 12,000 drawings required for the production of the 'prototype' were produced in some 147,000 man-hours by more than 70 draughtsmen under the direction of the Chief Draughtsman, A.G. Parkes. Among the draughtsmen was one of author Joseph Conrad's two sons.

The only prints known to exist are those of Drawing No S.23.C.29.013, a long section through the 'boat forming part of the Type Record showing the interior layout of the Mk II S.23 (the 'Bermuda' flying boat).

The drawing negatives were stored at Rochester until the Seaplane Works closed in 1948, when they were transferred to Belfast as part of the general move to Northern Ireland. Storage space in Ireland became increasingly scarce, and the negatives, as well as all remaining prints, were subsequently incinerated. Burnt too were all the calculations from the Stress Office; almost everything went up in flames. Part of the Type Record documents (discovered 1993) miraculously survived the inferno, shut away in a cupboard. The paperwork of the Type Record, but sadly without any accompanying drawings, is now safely lodged at the RAF Museum at Hendon.

The construction method for the hull shadowed traditional shipbuilding practice. Hulls were built round frames in stocks or gantries. The first 42 of the 51 frame positions in an Empire hull were built in gantries. Key frame positions were at Frame 6, the aft extent of the coupé, Frames 15/16, the forward mainplane double spar frame, and Frames 20/21, the aft mainplane spar frame; the aft step was at Frame 34 and the construction joint at Frame 42. All the material used in the hull was fabricated from British Aluminium Co. Ltd Alclad DTD 275 plate.

Hand drills were Desoutter 'Mighty Atom' 3/16 in diameter drills, supplied from galvanised steel tube compressed air lines, draped over the gantry framework, to outlet points around the gantry. The air compressors were at the back of No 3 Shop. Because the air driers took some time to become effective, the air pressure at the start of a shift on cold and foggy mornings was often low.

Broomwade pneumatic one-shot riveting guns were used for most of the rivets, the remainder being hand-closed. Hand-closed rivets were drawn up in the hole with one tool, and the tail snapped over inside to close the rivet down with another, so that the rivet head was flush with the surface of the plate. A flat metal 'dolly' was held up to the rivet head as it was being closed, usually by one of the many 'dolly' boys. Most of the plates, by careful design, were either flat or of single curvature. Plates of more complex form required more extensive shaping on wheeling machines, to be checked on timber jigs before being finally fixed. When all the plates had been fixed and the rivets closed down, the inner chine angle, the external chine angle and the keel buttstrap were fitted and riveted, to complete the hull.

Notices were hung on the gantries warning that only plimsoles – rubber-soled shoes, or trainers – could be worn by anyone working on the hulls.

The centre line of the gantry, and the completed aircraft, was marked by a painted line on the floor and used for locating and plumbing the keel board and top profile boards. The top profile board was fixed to the cross members of the gantry with angle brackets at each crossing, and had fixing brackets at each frame station. The positioning jig for Frame 42, the last hull frame in the gantry, was braced off the supporting framework. At various stages of the construction of a hull, tubular steel scaffolding was used inside the gantry structure, threaded transversely through the aircraft's frames, windows, ports (portholes),

also put in place. After alignment, Frame 42 was then bolted to the jig at the end of the gantry.

The hull frames were channel-shaped components, 2in wide. They were marked out from templates, rough cut with pneumatic hand shears, machine-pressed or hand-flanged from plate, drilled to detail on mild steel drilling templates, and checked for truth on a layout table. Tolerances were the same as for the keelson. They were then anodised and finally riveted up.

Frames 10 to 34 were stiffened by doubling up the channels, back to back. The doubling extended from the chine line to just above the line of the upper deck for Frames 10 to 14 and 17 to 19, or its equivalent for Frames 22 to 34. Frames 6, 11, 25, 29 and 34 had watertight bulkheads up to floor level.

Frames 1 to 14 and 22 to 36 were lowered into position along the keelson at their respective frame stations and temporarily fixed to the angle brackets of the top profile board and the keelson at the bottom. Using Frame 42 as the datum, the frames were aligned, trued up and plumbed to true vertical, working forward along the length of the hull. After inspection, the frames were clamped longitudinally along the outside of the hull with ¾in steel angle spacing bars to prevent the frames from moving while the stiffeners and stringers were fitted.

and hatches, to enable work to be carried out anywhere on the hull.

The keelson was about 62ft long, with a variable depth of between 4in and 5in along its length. The keelson stretched from the stem of the 'boat back to Frame 36, two frames aft of the rear step. From Frame 36 to Frame 48, two pressed Z sections acted in place of the keelson as supports for the frames and the keel buttstrap.

Completed keelsons were placed in position on the keel board in the gantry and clamped in position. The two Z section members that acted as dual keelsons from Frames 36 to 42, were

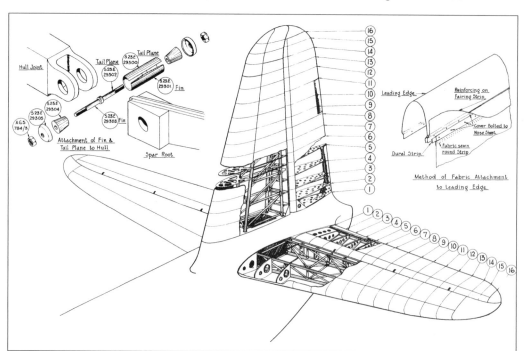

RIGHT **Tail unit.**
(Shorts)

The frames were then riveted to the keelson. As successive frames were fixed, the keelson was finally riveted in place between them.

The two double main spar frames, Frames 15/16 and 20/21, were assembled on flat table jigs as a sandwich of two plate frames substantially reinforced with angle and top-hat section pressings, kept apart with distance pieces. Both the main spar frames had watertight bulkheads up to floor level. The centre part of the mainplane spar trusses was built into the tops of the spar frames.

The aft part of the hull, starting at Frame 42, was made up as an assembly consisting of six single hull frames, and the two double spar frames, Frames 44/46 and 47/48, connected to the fin and tailplanes. The single frames were made from channel section in a similar way to the other hull frames, and assembled on a keelboard in the little gantry in No 11 Shop. The tailplane and fin spar frames were cut from blanks and assembled on table jigs, with the forged and machined S 80 steel jointing lugs sandwiched between. This sub-assembly was mated with the hull by bolting through the matching Frame 42 of the hull, forming a double frame. The joint was sheeted over during the cladding of the hull.

Hull stiffeners were intercostal between frames following the standard Short Bros'

technique of leaving the hull frames unnotched. About 3,000 stiffeners were used in a hull. Each stiffener was cut to length and the ends finished to the correct angle in a template. All details were anodised.

The top profile board was removed in sections as the sheeting of the top of the hull progressed. When sufficient plates had been fixed to make the hull stable, the keel board was removed and the hull jacked up to allow the shop truck to be inserted for removal from the gantry. The completed hull, perched on the truck, could then be withdrawn from the gantry. The aft part of the hull framing back from

ABOVE This image shows the construction of the tailplane of _Maia_, which was similar to that of an Empire, although the latter was smaller. The spans differed – _Maia_ 38ft and an Empire 32ft 1.3in; the relative areas were _Maia_ 283sq ft and an Empire 185sq ft. _(Shorts)_

FAR LEFT The spar box for the tailplane of _Maia_. The structure for an Empire was similar except for the spans. _(Shorts)_

LEFT Fin and tail-plane of _Maia_. _(Shorts)_

ABOVE The first two S.23 hulls being assembled in Gantries Nos 2 and 3. The hull in Gantry No 1, on the left of the picture, is that of *Maia*. As the hull in Gantry No 3 is the more advanced with the stiffeners in place, it is likely to be for *Canopus*. The hull in Gantry No 2 is that of *Caledonia*. The Empire 'boat hulls ended at Frame 42, the construction joint between the hull and the tail unit. The profile board for the third S.23 hull can just be seen to the right of the photograph. *(Shorts)*

BELOW An interior view of a fully framed hull, looking forwards. The cross-braced frame, at 21/22, is the connection with the aft mainplane spar. *(Shorts)*

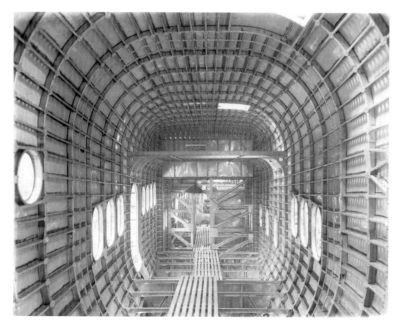

Frame 42 was sometimes bolted in position before the hull was withdrawn, or later before the skin plating was fixed. The hull remained on the shop truck until the beaching chassis was attached, just before the final roll-out. A 90° left turn faced the 'boat on the centre line of the exit doors while the remainder of the work was carried out.

Before the skin plating was fixed to the hull, the remaining detail fittings were fixed in position on the skeleton of the hull, including the coamings for the hatches, windows, and ports.

Skin plating

Five different thicknesses of DTD 275 sheet were used for plating the hull and planing bottom. Approximately 300 sheets, with an area of about 3,000sq ft were needed to plate a hull. The thickness of 22 plates of the strengthened 'boats was increased from 20 SWG to 18 SWG.

Hull plating was arranged in strakes across the frames approximately parallel to the waterline. Plating laps and seams were joggled. Most hull plates spanned two frames, with the occasional three, and four, frame plate. The planing bottom was plated with two different thicknesses of sheet, 18 SWG from the stem to Frame 10, toothing into 16 SWG sheet to the main step.

From the main to the rear step, the bottom was in 18 SWG sheet. Watertight hull riveting extended from the planing bottom upwards to the upper seam of the strake that started in the nose with Plate 'ai' to Plate 'ah' in the tail.

Plates were cut to exact size, repositioned on the hull and held with ³⁄₃₂in temporary bolts, each with a ½in diameter red fibre washer to protect the anodising. The remainder of the rivet holes in the plate were drilled back through the stiffeners. Plates with thicknesses of 18 SWG or thicker, were countersunk to take the rivet heads flush. The holes in thinner plates were dimpled with a special hand-lever tool, as were the corresponding holes in the stiffeners.

Each plate was then taken down once more, the holes de-burred, buffed and the plate anodised. The frames and stiffeners were painted with Duralac jointing compound, the newly anodised plates were put up to the frame and stiffeners, temporarily bolted in position, tack riveted and closed down. The temporary bolts were removed, and the remaining rivets inserted and closed down, to complete the fixing of the plate.

The S.23, S.30 and S.33 'boats, without the flight refuelling hull, had the tail light housing fitted, the tail cap (plates 'dr' and 'cn' – port and starboard), fitted and fixed. The S.23 and S.30 'boats with flight refuelling hulls, had the tail cup fitted to Frame 51, with the trap door immediately below it in place of the standard tail cap. The

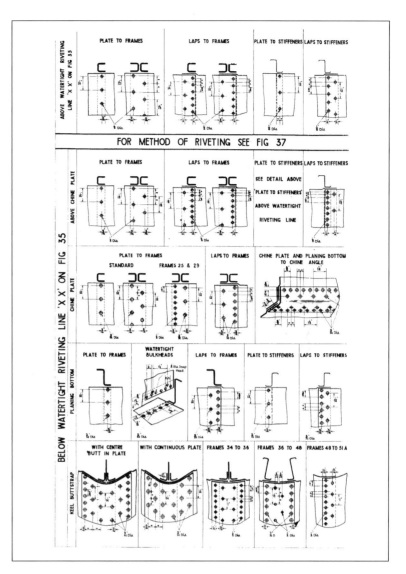

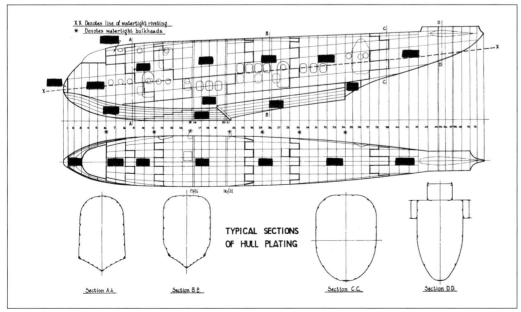

ABOVE Empire 'boat hull construction, showing the different riveting patterns and types of joints. *(Shorts)*

LEFT Typical sections of hull plating for an Empire 'boat. *(Shorts)*

Shorts S.23 'C' class Empire flying boat.

(Mike Badrocke)

1 Starboard elevator
2 Tailplane construction
3 Elevator tab
4 Tail navigation light
5 Tail cone
6 Rudder tabs
7 Fabric-covered rudder construction
8 Fin girder construction
9 Leading edge construction
10 Aerial cable
11 Port fabric-covered elevator
12 Port tailplane
13 Rudder and elevator control levers
14 Tailplane attachment double frames
15 Fuselage frame and stringer construction
16 Construction joint Frame 42
17 Rear bulkhead
18 Baggage door
19 Aft main baggage bay
20 Cabin rear bulkhead
21 Window panels
22 Bilge keel construction
23 Aft cabin seating, six passengers
24 Cabin trim panels
25 Overhead luggage racks
26 Rear entry door
27 Bulkhead doorway
28 Wing root trailing edge fillet
29 Cabin roof bedding stowage
30 Window curtains
31 Wing root rib

32 Starboard aerial mast
33 Promenade cabin, eight passengers
34 Starboard flap shroud
35 Starboard Gouge-type flap
36 Girder construction rear spar
37 Trailing edge ribs
38 Starboard aileron
39 Fixed tab
40 Aileron control horns
41 Wing tip fairing
42 Starboard navigation light
43 Wire-braced wing rib construction
44 Front girder spar
45 Leading edge nose ribs
46 Float mounting struts
47 Diagonal wire bracing
48 Starboard wing tip float construction
49 Landing/taxiing lamp
50 Wing stringers
51 Over-wing exhaust outlet
52 Carburettor air intake
53 Starboard outer engine nacelle construction

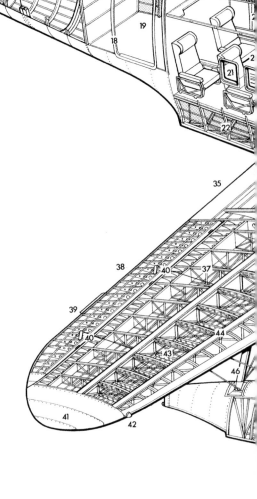

SHORT 'C' CLASS SPECIFICATIONS

S.23 **Power plant:** 4 x Bristol Pegasus X nine-cylinder radial engines each rated at 740bhp at 3,500ft (1,067m).
Performance: Max speed, 200mph at 5,500ft; cruising speed using 500bhp per engine, 165mph; stalling speed, 73mph; rate of climb at sea level, 950ft/min; absolute ceiling, 20,000ft; still-air range, normal tankage, 760 miles.
Weights: Empty, 24,000lb; fuel (600gal) 4,560lb; oil (44gal) 400lb; equipment, 3,340lb; payload and crew of five, 8,200lb; initial max gross, 40,500lb.
Dimensions: Span, 114ft; length, 88ft; height, 31ft 10in; wing area, 1,500sq ft.

S.30 **Power plant:** 4 x Bristol Perseus XIIC sleeve-valve radial engines each rated at 700bhp at 3,500ft.
Performance: Speed as for S.23; still-air range, normal tankage, 1,870 miles.
Weights: Empty, 27,825lb; normal max gross, 46,000lb; air-refuelled gross, 53,000lb.
Dimensions: As for S.23.

S.33 **Power plant:** 4 x Bristol Pegasus XI engines.
Performance, weights and dimensions: As for S.23.

54 Engine mounting ring
55 Exhaust collector ring
56 Detachable engine cowlings
57 Oil cooler radiators
58 Hull planning bottom forward
   step
59 Midships cabin, three
   passengers
60 Midships window panel
61 Starboard inner engine
   nacelle
62 Cooling air flaps
63 Nacelle tail fairing
64 Heater intake duct
65 Cabin heater/exhaust heat
   exchanger
66 Wing/fuselage main spar
   attachments
67 Root rib cut-outs
68 Wing spar centre section
   carry-through
69 Port Gouge-type trailing edge
   flap
70 Flap screw jack
71 Port aerial mast
72 Flap guide rails

73 Port aileron
74 Aileron control cables
75 Fixed tab
76 Port wing tip fairing
77 Port navigation light
78 Front girder spar
79 Port outer engine nacelle
80 Oil tank
81 Bristol Pegasus XC air-
   cooled nine-cylinder radial
   engine
82 De Havilland three-bladed
   propeller
83 Rotol hub
84 Port wing tip float
85 Ram air intakes
86 Oil radiators
87 Outboard main fuel tanks
88 Port inner engine nacelle
89 Exhaust collector ring
90 Cooling air flaps
91 Over-wing exhaust outlet

92 Exhaust pipe heat exchanger
93 Inboard main fuel tank; total
   capacity 600 Imp. gal
94 Engine cowl flaps and fuel
   cock controls
95 Ship's clerk station
96 Mail loading hatch
97 Access ladder between
   decks
98 Steward's galley
99 Port side toilet doors,
   two toilets
100 Upper deck level

101 Port mail and freight
    compartment
102 Sliding door
103 Forward entry door
104 Smoking lounge, seven
    passengers
105 Fuselage chine member
106 Forward fuselage portholes
107 Radio operator's seat

108 Radio racks
109 Aerial mast
110 Pitot tubes
111 Cockpit roof hatch
112 Chart table
113 Cockpit roof trim control
    cables
114 Captain's seat
115 Sliding cockpit side
    windows
116 First Officer's seat
117 Control column
118 Rudder pedals
119 Instrument panel shroud
120 Curved windscreen panels
121 Mooring hatch
122 Marine equipment
    compartment
123 Mooring ladder
124 Anchor winch
125 Anchor stowage
126 Retractable mooring bollard
127 Towing cleat

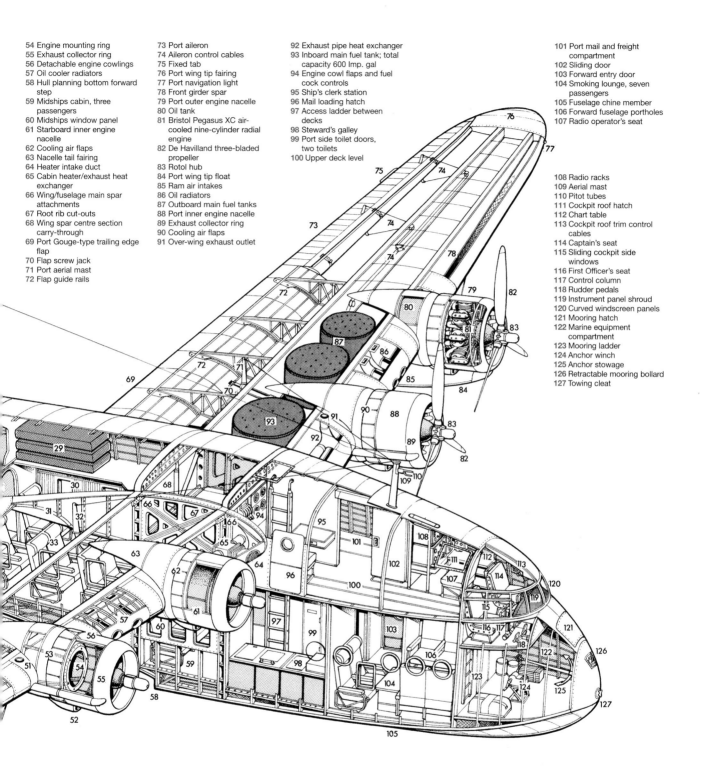

S.30 'boats also had a hatch and wedge plate for fixing the KBB drift sight in the afterbody of the hull, aft of the stowage floor of the freight room. The S.30 flight-refuelled aircraft had small sheet acetate windows let into the skin plating on both sides of the aircraft between Frames 40 and 41.

The fin and tailplanes were of similar construction, based on the constructional method evolved for the mainplane of the Scion. The rudder had a lead mass balance weight of 16lb 10oz in the leading edge, 7ft 2.76in up from the junction with the hull. The upper tab in the trailing edge, between Ribs 8 and 11, was a servo to help in moving the rudder. The lower tab, between Ribs 2 and 5, was a trim tab. Both these tabs were formed from solid mahogany on brass hinges.

The normal riveting pitches for $\frac{1}{8}$in diameter rivets were:

plates to single frames	1½in single seam
plates to double frames	1½in double reeled
plate laps to single and double	
frames double seam	1½in
plates to stiffeners	1½in single seam
plate laps to stiffeners	
double seam	1½in and ¾in

The control surfaces of the rudder and elevators, aft of their respective spars, were covered with 4oz/sq yd long-fibred flax cloth to BSS F.1. A doped-on, doubled-over, frayed-edge reinforcing strip finished the trailing edge, covering the stitching.

The transparencies for the windows and ports were cut from Rhodoid cellulose acetate sheet. The ports (portholes), windows and bunk windows for the first 25 'boats were fixed. From the 26th 'boat, *Coogee*, onwards, all the windows in the passenger cabins could be pushed out as emergency exits, and instructions for use were attached to each window. The first 25 'boats were retro-fitted with push-out windows. The brackets on the walls for the parcel racks and fittings for the bunks, and parcel rack straps on the ceilings, were all fixed in position.

After inspection, the skin plating joints were tested with a high-pressure water hose. On completion of the test, the hull was pumped out and allowed to dry. Any defective rivets were drilled out and re-riveted.

Coupé

The roof, windscreen, and sliding direct-vision windows of the control deck forward of Frame 6 were built as a unit, known at Rochester as the coupé, and usually attached to the hull after it had been withdrawn from the gantry. The windscreen was provided with sliding direct-vision panels on both sides. The transparencies were fabricated from heat-formed Rhodoid cellulose acetate sheet (V13B grade) and inserted into the frames with black Bostick C adhesive and Bostick glazing compound. The coupé was water tested by hose after assembly. The visibility from the pilots' seats through the ample windscreen, forwards and to the sides, was extensive: 'excellent' was Captain J.C. Kelly-Rogers' description. The curvature of the windscreen did not require screen wipers.

The noise levels on the control decks of Empire 'boats and the Boeing 314As were comparable, although the level of vibration on the 314As was more noticeable. The control decks of the two 'A' flying boats were insulated when the cabin heating arrangements were changed in late 1944 or early 1945. The coupé on the Short Sandringham VH-BRC, on display in the Solent Sky Museum at Southampton, is an S.23 coupé installed during the conversion from Sunderland status.

Once the coupé was in place on the hull, the controls for the flaps and the trim tabs could be fitted to the underside of the coupé on the aircraft's centre line.

The elevator trim tab mechanism was fitted to the roof, with the operating handles accessible to both pilots. The quadrants of the operating box were marked 'elevator trim nose up nose down'. The nose down movement was put on by turning the handles forward, 6.38 turns being required to move the trim tab through its full movement. Turning the handles aft brought the nose up. A pointer moved along the sides of the operating box to show the degree of trim.

The single rudder trim tab control handle was facing downwards, accessible to both pilots. The quadrant was marked 'rudder trim', 'turn left', and 'turn right'. Trim was applied by turning the handle, 7.74 turns either way for the

full extent of the tab. The handle operated in the natural sense, marked on the rudder trim plate. The degree of trim was indicated by a pointer that moved in a slot in the casing.

The flap controls were mounted on the underside of the roof. The Rotax N5 EC three-position 'controller flaps' operating switch, the 'on/off' flap motor switch, the flap position indicator and the red and blue indicator lights were grouped together. The blue light indicated 'on/off'. When the flap reached the 'out' position, the red indicator light came on until the flap reached the same point as it retracted.

The tail slip release hook operating handle was also mounted on the underside of the coupé roof, slightly to starboard of the centre line. The spring-loaded release required a single pull to free the tail slip line. The Sandringham at Southampton still has the operating handle in position.

Roller sunblinds were fitted to cover each side of the windscreen. A blind was also fitted across the control deck behind the pilots' seats for use when flying at night, and one was fitted to the port that lit the radio officer's desk.

The frames for the pilots' seats were fixed to the floor structure, and adjustable seats installed. Safety restraint harnesses for the pilots were provided, which proved somewhat restricting in use. The seats were adjustable up and down in five increments, each of 2in. By lifting the cross tube below the front edge, the seat could be moved backwards or forwards in increments of 2in. The seats were fitted with leather-covered seat and back cushions and flip-up arm rests.

Each pilot had a complete control column unit consisting of hand-wheel, column, and base. The hand-wheel, devoid of switches, had a turn of 87° each way and a fore-and-aft movement of 15° 40' each way, the neutral position being vertical.

ABOVE Pilots' instrument panel and central control console. *(Shorts)*

Instrument panel

A three-panel pilots' instrument panel was mounted clear of the airframe on Lord shock absorbers, just forward of Frame 4. The centre panel, immediately over the throttle box, included the controls for the automatic pilot. The port and starboard sides of the panel contained the following standard flying instruments:

1 Captain and First Officer control columns
2 Captain and First Officer rudder pedals
3 Throttles
4 Mixture controls
5 The 'gate'
6 Pitch controls
7 Engine ignition switches
8 Sperry panel containing Sperry directional gyro and artificial horizon
9 Compass
10 3.75in Smiths AV 549 air speed indicator (mph)
11 Rate of climb indicator

12 Turn indicator
13 Trip clock
14 3.5in Sperry artificial horizon
15 Smiths AV 875 fore-and-aft level
16 Four 2.12in oil pressure gauges (one for each engine)
17 Two Record Cirscale engine speed indicators (one for each pair of engines, port and starboard)
18 Two boost gauges (port and starboard engine pairs) and two engine selector cocks. Later aircraft were fitted with a boost gauge for each individual engine
19 Smiths turn and bank indicator
20 3.75in Smiths AV 567 static altimeter
21 The data plates included the Pegasus engine and the Sperry automatic pilot plates
22 Engine cut-out levers
23 Automatic pilot engaging lever
24 Engine starter buttons

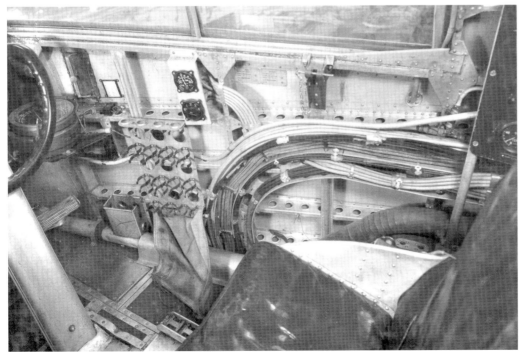

ABOVE Flight deck, Captain's side – controls and instruments. *(Shorts)*

1 Trailing aerial drum
2 Pitot head heater switches
3 Bow searchlight control levers – top lever is UP/DOWN, lower lever IN/OUT
4 Bow searchlight, docking, steaming and landing light switches
5 Sperry autopilot control panel
6 Instrument panel lighting switchboard

LEFT Flight deck, First Officer's side – (from left) compass, clips for signalling cartridges, and external air temperature gauge. *(Shorts)*

Temperature gauge panel

The temperature gauge panel was situated behind the first officer's right shoulder, on the starboard side of the aircraft, between Frames 6 and 7. This panel carried the following instruments for Pegasus-engined aircraft with Sperry automatic pilot:

- Weston Pyrometer Model 602 HJ 509 engine cylinder-head temperature indicator, 0 to 350°C, with a Weston four-way rotary switch. The twin copper-constantan cables ran from the four-way switch to the junction box in each engine nacelle, and from there to a Bristol thimble couple on the No 1 cylinder of each engine.
- Four 2.12in oil temperature gauges – one for each engine.

BELOW Smith Mk IA automatic pilot.
(Shorts)

- Four 2.12in carburettor air intake thermometers – one for each engine.
- Vacuum distributor, gauge, adjuster and control cocks for the Sperry automatic pilot connected to the Romec vacuum pumps on the two starboard engines.

Fitted above the automatic pilot panel were the engine ignition switches and the starter buttons. Each pair of magnetos to an engine was controlled by a switch knob, yoked together in pairs for port and starboard. The four Rotax N5 CD engine starter buttons were on the top of the panel, protected by a flip-up cover. The starter solenoid circuit cables ran from the connection box on the main switchboard, through the Tucker B 70 two-way switch and the Rotax SFS Type N5EB fuse, to the buttons of the flush-mounted Lundberg twin-knob starter switch units.

Clyde and *Clare* were fitted with air speed indicators registering in knots, with a repeater and outside air thermometer at the navigation table.

Compasses for both pilots were Smith PL 4s, Hughes P/4/11s, or Kelvin, Bottomley & Baird KBB 4s Type PL 4 mounted immediately aft of the respective dashboard panel.

Centre panel and controls

The centre panel of the dashboard, immediately over the throttle box, contained the control panel for the Sperry Gyropilot for all the 'boats except S.30 'A' aircraft equipped with a Smith Mk 1A automatic pilot. The Sperry control unit comprised the directional gyro unit, the bank and climb gyro unit, and the vacuum gauge. The autopilot engaging lever was a Bowden double pull lever, located above the airscrew pitch control levers on the rear of the throttle box (lever to port 'off', lever to starboard 'on').

The Sperry speed valves (graduated from 0 to 6) and oil pressure gauge (graduated from 0 to 300psi) were mounted on the port side of the control deck, immediately forward of the bow searchlight controls. Captain Kelly-Rogers' comment was that they had a habit of dribbling down the pilot's left trouser leg.

The airscrew pitch controls were at the aft end of the throttle box, below the Sperry automatic pilot lever, near the floor. The

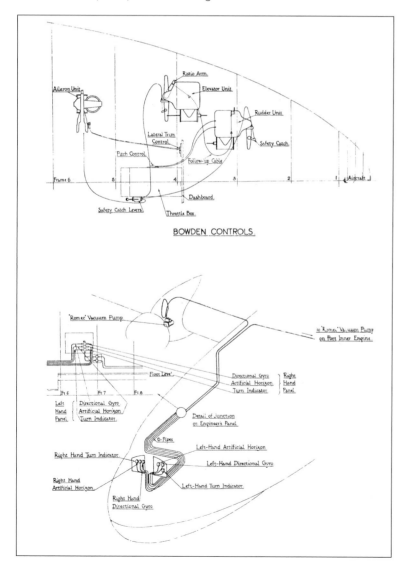

airscrews of the Pegasus-engined 'boats were controlled by a two-position lever (red knobs for port engines, green knobs for starboard engines, 'up' for coarse, 'down' for fine pitch). For the S.30 'boats with Perseus engines, Exactor units were used for the pitch control (increase revolutions 'up', decrease 'down').

The two engine cut-out control levers were mounted either side of the throttle box (inner engines port side lever, outer engines starboard side lever). The levers operated spring-loaded valves cutting off the supply of fuel to the slow-running jets of the carburettors, stopping the engines dead when pulled.

The carburettor test cock controls were located between the pilots' seats below a section of flooring, hinged along the aft edge, and lifted by a ring-pull let into the top surface. Each engine had a lever ('red' for port, 'green' for starboard) operating a pulley round which a 10cwt W2/5 stranded steel wire cable ran over pulleys to each carburettor.

The controls for the retractable bow 'landing searchlight' were mounted just below the windscreen coaming on the captain's side at Frame 5. The dual Teleflex remote control levers

moved the light 'in/out' or 'up/down'.

The aerial mast was mounted on the centre line of the hull, just aft of Frame 9, and besides mounting the pitot head, it contained the extending mast for the pennants and national flags, with the anchor and steaming light housing on top.

Berco Type BE 5630 instrument heaters were fitted to the port and starboard dashboard panels – two each side. The switches for the instrument heaters and the two Kollsman Type 171B pressure heads were labelled 'pressure heads' and 'dashboard', with the indicator lights on the port instrument panel. The instrument lighting sub-board was on the port side of the aircraft, beside the captain's seat.

Fuel tanks and systems

The S.23 Empire 'boats with Bristol Pegasus XC engines were the first British commercial aircraft to use 87-octane aviation spirit to the DTD 230 specification. The spirit derived from petroleum, with added aromatics and/or tetraethyl lead, and had a specific gravity of about 0.76 depending on the exact origin of

BELOW Fuel system.

(Shorts)

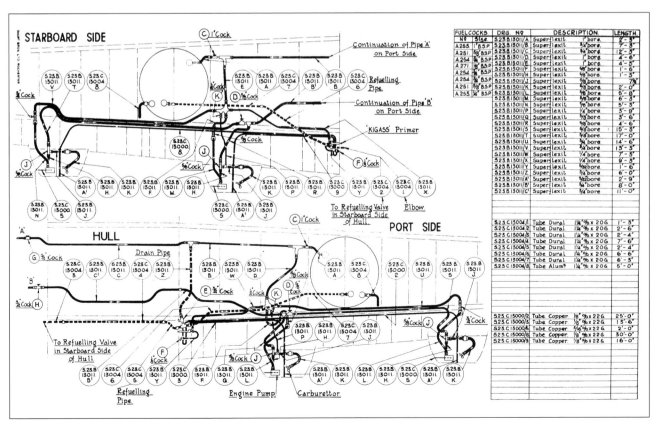

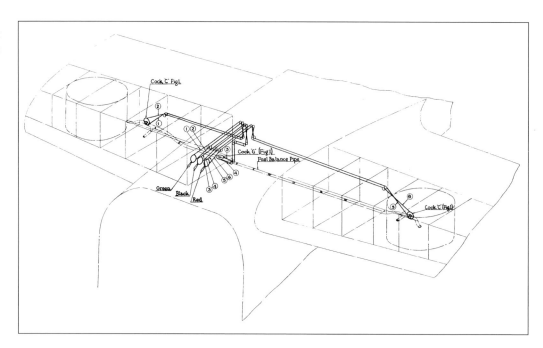

the base stock, but was often shown on the aircraft weight schedules as 0.74. The boiling point of the spirit was between 50 and 180°C, which caused some problems with vapour locks in the fuel systems in the hotter ports along the route. Aircraft with Pegasus XXII engines used 100-octane spirit.

It was IAL policy that no fuel tanks should be fitted in the hulls of the passenger-carrying 'boats. It was only the ultra-long-range Types 1B and M1, with their eight and nine tank arrays, that had tanks installed in the hull between the wing spars over the centre cabin, and the small top-up tank on the control deck.

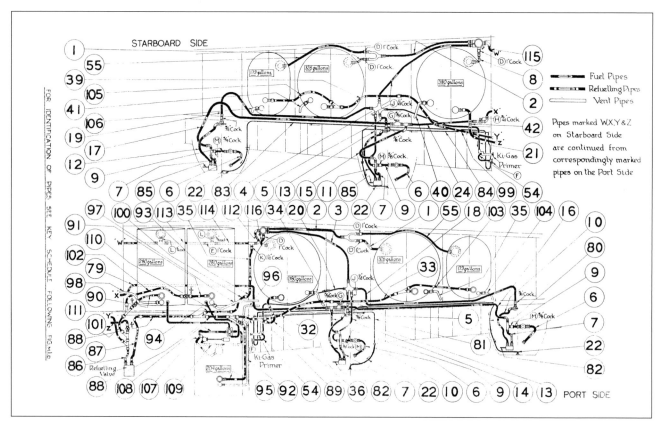

Tank positions were:

Wing	mid-position	326gal	wing
	inboard	380gal	wing
	outboard	179gal	wing
Hull		280gal	between spar frames
Control deck			
	top-up M1	204gal	on the port side

Seven 'boats were fitted with 1B and M1 fuel systems with two 280gal tanks located in the hull between Frames 15/16 and 20/21, installed on bearers over the centre cabin. The five S.30 aircraft with M1 fuel systems – the four S.30 flight-refuelled 'boats *Cabot, Caribou, Connemara* and *Clyde,* and the rebuilt *Australia* as *Clare* had the additional smaller top-up tank on the control deck.

Wartime operations brought more informal tank arrangements. *Cathay* and *Champion* arrived in Durban in January 1943 to join the Horseshoe Route with three 120gal tanks in the centre cabin, plumbed in with domestic stop valves and sight glasses. A18-13 *Coolangatta* was modified with rails in the promenade cabin, enabling it to carry 'several' Australian Wirraway

aircraft tanks strapped down. With this tankage it could refuel itself on the open sea. In December 1941, *Corsair* was recorded with an 'extra 100gal tank', location unknown.

AGS fuel filters were originally installed in the supply lines, immediately upstream of the engine pumps, fixed to a convenient vertical

LEFT A fold-down maintenance platform in the wing leading edge in its open position, ready to facilitate maintenance work. *(Shorts)*

BELOW Tank cock controls 2,534gal. *(Shorts)*

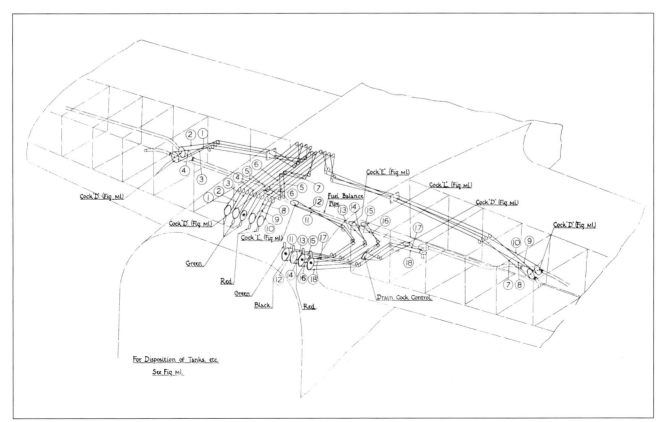

ABOVE *Caledonia*'s starboard long-range wing with fuel tanks installed ready for lifting for attachment to the hull. The starboard half mainplane of *Centaurus* is next in the line, with another port half mainplane spar box behind it. In the gantries are, left to right, the hulls of the Sunderland prototype *K4774*, *Cambria* and *Cygnus*. *(Shorts)*

joined with De Bergue patent rivets, with an interleaving of petrol-resisting tape in the joint.

Each tank was fitted with a Relunits float-operated shut-off valve at the inlet. The tank vent acted as overflow to discharge at the under surface of the nearest mainplane. Tanks were fitted with a single 1½in-diameter cast light-alloy outlet sump, protected with a low vertical baffle fixed concentrically around the sump outlet on the bottom of the tank. The baffle was slotted to allow the spirit to reach the sump.

The fuel tank contents gauges were either Telelevel or KDG Korect gauges. The Telelevel equipment was mechanically operated and used on all the 'boats up to *Cathay*. *Cathay* and subsequent 'boats were fitted with KDG Korect electrically signalled floating-arm equipment.

Mainplanes

The Empire was the third Short Bros design for a monoplane flying boat. The span of 114ft was constant for all types of Empire 'boat – S.23, S.30, and S.33. The gross area of the mainplanes for all types was 1,720sq ft, with a net area excluding the flaps, ailerons, and nacelles of 1,510sq ft, normally quoted as 1,500sq ft. The aspect ratios were respectively 7.56 and 8.60. The datum chord was 16ft 5.5in at a point 23ft 11.32in from the centre line of the aircraft at right angles to the plane of symmetry. The AD 5 (modified Gö 436) aerofoil used had a thickness to chord ratio of 18.78% at the junction with the hull, diminishing to a hypothetical 9% thickness to chord ratio at the tip. There was no washout. Each half-plane was 52ft long, with a chord of 21ft 0.327in at the junction with the hull.

Spar box and booms

The mainplanes were built in two halves, port and starboard, around a massive spar box. There were three designs for the half-mainplane, short, medium, and long range depending on which of the fuel systems it had to accommodate.

The spar box was formed by a forward and aft spar boom connected by drag struts and braced with incidence bracing wires. The spar booms were in the form of Parker girders, with extruded light-alloy T-section top and bottom

BELOW **Starboard mainplane showing the modified Gö 436 profile and the housing for the Gouge flaps.** *(Shorts)*

member of the forward mainplane spar boom, accessible through the maintenance platforms in the leading edge. A shut-off cock was installed in the line to allow the filter to be cleaned. Following incidences of vapour locking, the filters were lowered.

Fuel tanks were fabricated from 18 SWG DTD 275 clad alloy sheet for the tops and bottoms, and 20 SWG for the side shells,

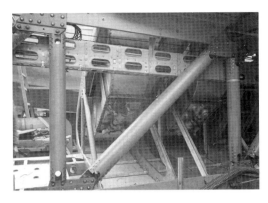

ABOVE A view from inside the port mainplane showing the forward spar, the back of an oil cooler, and the maintenance platform in the open position. *(Shorts)*

ABOVE A mainplane spar being assembled. Each side of the mainplane was built from a jig in the centre simulating the width of the hull, known in the Shop as 'Westminster bridge'. The two spar trusses, fore and aft, were joined to form a box. *(Shorts)*

members in 22ft lengths. Three extrusions were joined to make up the flange of a spar boom, two full-length extrusions and the third, 4ft long.

The largest spar box section (top of the forward boom) was 4in wide by 5in deep, with a flange thickness of 0.655in. The smallest was 2in by 1.53in, with a flange thickness of 0.17in. The corresponding flange sections for the bottom boom were 4in by 3.807in by 0.507in, and 2.07in by 1.45in by 0.17in. The alloy sections for the rear booms were slightly smaller.

The spar boom flange sections were machined to constant tapers in width, depth, and thickness throughout their length on a modified horizontal milling machine installed in No 9 Machine Shop. The machine was modified by extending the travelling table from 10ft 6in to the full length of an extrusion. Other machines were bought and modified during the Second World War, and at least one was transferred to the safety of tunnels excavated in the chalk behind No 18 Shop, so the production of Sunderland spar booms could continue undisturbed by air raids. The flanges were milled to a taper, a constant 1:132, for the length of a complete spar boom.

Mainplane components

Each half-plane was divided into six principal components – the spar box, the leading-edge ribs and covering, the trailing-edge ribs and covering, the engine nacelles, the flap, and the

LEFT Wing under construction showing internal spars. *(Shorts)*

aileron. The surviving Type Record documents refer to the stress calculations for two spar loadings – 39,000lb and 40,500lb take-off weights. The time limit on the Empire 'boat mainplane spars was set at 13,250 flying hours. By 31 May 1945, *Canopus* had 12,794hr in the logbook, and there were four more of the surviving 'boats with similar hours. In the final reckoning, when they came to be scrapped, four of the BOAC 'boats had exceeded the limit with more than 15,000hr, and one had 14,989hr. Empire 'boats were later refuelled in flight to all-up weights of 53,000lb and later took off at this weight. The hulls of the S.30 and S.33 'boats were strengthened but there is no mention, in any of the records, of wing spar modification or strengthening.

The 16 lift struts and verticals were alloy tubes, slotted to detail in the Machine Shop before going to the Spar Detail Shop at the rear of No 3 Shop to be jig-drilled before fixing. The tubes ranked down from a maximum of 3.5in outside diameter by 13 SWG to 1in by 20 SWG. The connections between the spar flanges and the lift struts were made with plug-ends extruded from L 40 alloy, shaped in the Machine Shop.

The two types of drag struts, that joined both top and bottom boom flanges of a spar truss,

were made up in the Spar Detail Shop. The majority were lighter intermediate struts, similar to ribs, built from L 40 extruded T-section top and bottom flanges, shaped to the aerofoil profile on rolling machines and checked against steel templates.

The built-up heavier box section struts were hand-flanged to channel sections and riveted to the top and bottom strut flanges. The top flanges of the upper struts were shaped to the aerofoil, but the lower struts were carefully curved to accommodate the load distribution and laminated with doublers, and in some places treblers, on the top chord. The side members were likewise laminated at the end bearings on the spar truss.

The diagonal incidence bracing between the two spar booms was by crossed, swaged streamline W 3 steel wires in pairs, on either side of a lift strut, except in positions where this interfered with a fuel tank. The wires varied in size from $5/16$in BSF at the first panel position outboard from the wing root, to 4 BA at the tip end of the spar. The wires ended with forked ends, pinned to shackles riveted to the spar boom webs.

The top skin of the spar box in DTD 275 alloy was fitted, drilled, anodised, and finally

BELOW Mainplane construction. *(Shorts)*

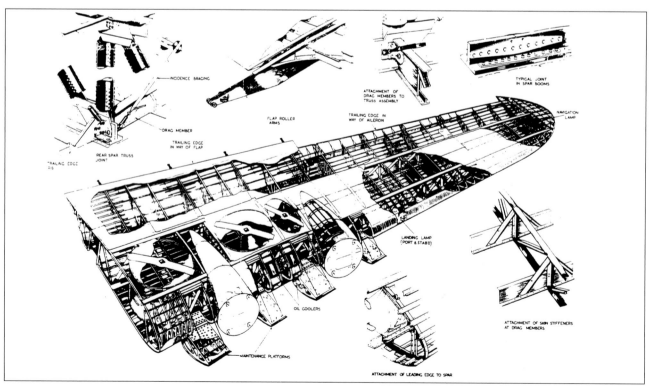

riveted, using the same procedure as for the hull plating. The thickness of the skin varied from 16 SWG for the first two boom panels outboard from the root, to 24 SWG at the tip end. The openings were cut and rebated into the top surface to receive the tank covers.

The tank positions were:

mid-position	326gal
inboard	380gal
outboard	179gal

The remainder of the skin plating was completed and the fuel tanks installed. The nacelles were attached, the controls run and the other equipment installed. Fuel tanks rested on grids made of spruce, spanning between the lower boom members of the front and rear spar trusses. The rubber-bushed anti-vibration bottom fitting of a tank was fixed to the substantial fore-and-aft spruce bearer that ran between the bottom members of the spar trusses.

The 34 leading edge ribs were cut from alloy sheet blanks. Ribs 3, 4, 5, 6, 9, and 10 were reinforced with a tubular brace for the maintenance platforms.

The structure of the trailing edge drag members, or ribs, depended on their function.

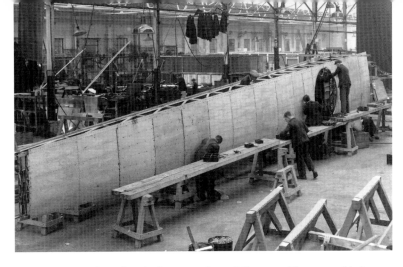

ABOVE The starboard mainplane spar box of *Canopus*. The assembly is tipped on to its leading edge as the sheeting between the spar booms is fixed. Most of the sheets are riveted, with three of them tack bolted. The rear spar boom is visible as are the top and bottom flanges protruding from the tip. *(Shorts)*

Working outboard from the hull, were four flap-support ribs, interspaced by four skin-support ribs and a special junction rib between the flap and the aileron. The flap-support ribs carried the sealed ball-races, which engaged in the channels on the top surface of the flap. Further sets of races were fixed at right angles to prevent the flaps from binding when they moved.

The completed ailerons were lifted into position and the hinge bolts bolted to the hinge

BELOW Aileron construction. *(Shorts)*

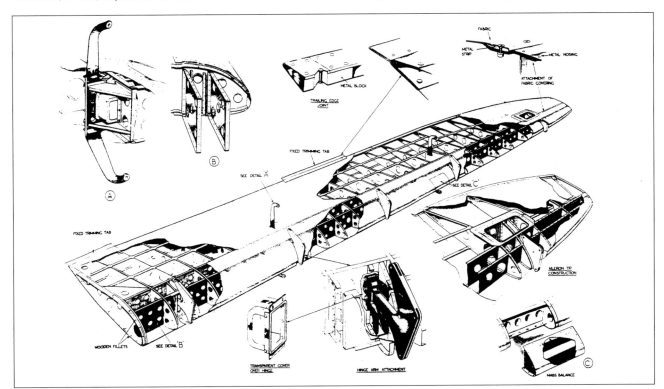

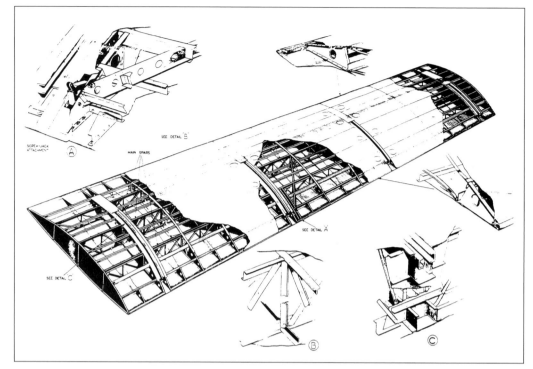

RIGHT Flap construction. *(Shorts)*

BELOW A port side mainplane flap ready for skinning on its upper surface. *(Shorts)*

BOTTOM Gouge flap housing beneath the trailing edge of the mainplane. *(Shorts)*

ribs. The covers at the hinges were secured with anchor nuts, and the tear-off fabric patches fitted. The aileron tie rods were $5/16$in diameter steel rods, passing through Tufnol blocks secured to light-alloy fairlead brackets, bolted through the webs of the main spar extrusions. Changes in direction in the control runs were in Reynolds steel chains over stainless steel sprockets with ball-bearing journals. The controls were then finally connected to the aileron levers through dashpots. A lead mass balance weight of 20lb 7oz was bolted in position in the leading edge at Rib 19, 47ft 4.56in out from the aircraft's centre line to prevent flutter.

The port and starboard flaps were assembled in jigs from details in DTD 275 alloy. The four hinge ribs in L 1 alloy that were runners for the flap guides, the five normal ribs, and the end ribs were assembled on the spar that ran in the centre of the flap. The jig also contained the V-shaped trailing edge, the stiffener channels, and the bottom 24 SWG skin plating.

The torque tubes operating the flap jacks were jointed with universal couplings running in ball-races. The torque tube drive ended by engaging with a worm and worm-wheel drive on the end of the jack. The worm gear rotated the jack casing, which forced out the square-threaded spindle to move the flap. The maximum extension of the jack was 30in, taking 6,250 revs of the standard flap motor to move the flap through an angle of 25°.

The port and starboard flaps were assembled in jigs from details. The four runners for the flap guides, the five normal ribs, and the end ribs were assembled on the spar that ran in the centre of the flap. The lug for the flap-operating jack was fixed to Hinge Rib No 3, the other end of the jack being fitted to the lower rear spar boom. The flaps were sheeted and drain holes drilled in the trailing edges.

The ailerons were assembled on jigs from DTD 275 alloy details. Each aileron consisted of a built-up box spar with a channelled web and 24 nose diaphragms. The aileron box spar was sheeted with 22 SWG sheet, beaten to shape over timber formers.

The engine nacelles were of monocoque construction. The frames were assembled on a jig and the various holes for oil tank access, engine starter handle, and fire extinguisher were cut and reinforced. The boundary frames were cut from 14 SWG sheet and beaten to shape on formers. The skin plating was attached, and the boundary angle at the junction of the nacelle and the aerofoil profile riveted in position. The nose spinning was then riveted in position and the work removed from the jig. The three-piece fire bulkhead and the Exactor control brackets were fitted. The top fairing was made ready for fixing after the nacelle had been mounted on the half-mainplane.

The completed half-mainplane was then ballasted with a quantity of lead shot at the root end to balance it, and slung with a four-strop sling for lifting by the bridge crane.

Attaching the half-mainplane

To attach a half-mainplane the root ends of the spar booms were temporarily secured with undersized bolts. The half-mainplane was jacked up to the correct dihedral by long steel adjustable jacking struts in the positions where the floats were later to be fixed. The dihedral was a little over 1° on the upper surface on the spar centre line. The jig plates were fitted to the spar boom flanges and the fixing holes were drilled with a special cutter 0.005in undersize, ready for reaming. The jig-plates were removed,

the biscuit plates refitted and reamed in position, and the stainless steel attachment bolts fitted. The six countersunk screws on the upper and lower surfaces of the spar booms were screwed home, and the detachable inboard nose bolted to the spar webs. The upper and lower light-alloy drag angles were bolted to the sides of the hull. The fabric strips at the leading edge and the upper and lower surfaces of the trailing edges were doped on. The leading edge fairing at the junction of the half-plane and hull was screwed in place, and the connections made for the various control functions inside the wing at the junction with the hull. The jacks supporting each half-mainplane were then struck.

ABOVE Sheeting the under-surface of a mainplane. *(Shorts)*

BELOW A port mainplane with flap section ready for fitting. *(Shorts)*

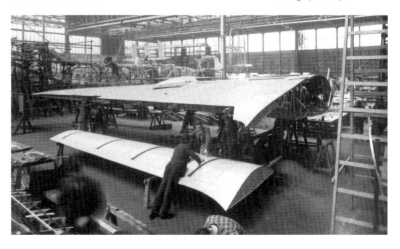

RIGHT Wing tip float construction. *(Shorts)*

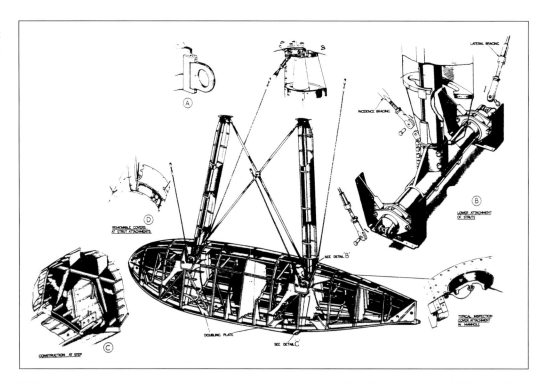

Floats

Three types of floats were fitted to the 'boats. Type 1, with a buoyancy of 6,000lb, was designed for *Maia*, the lower part of the Short–Mayo composite aircraft. Type 2, with a buoyancy of 5,000lb, was fitted to the S.23 'boats. The Type 2 float was revised with a

more streamlined form for the S.30 'boats. The floats were interchangeable with each other and with S.25 Sunderlands.

Five frames and four bulkheads were required for a Type 2 float, with an extra frame for a Type 1 float. A bilging tube extended from a bilge pump connection on the top of the float between each pair of bulkheads, extending

BELOW Plane tip float and chassis. *(Shorts)*

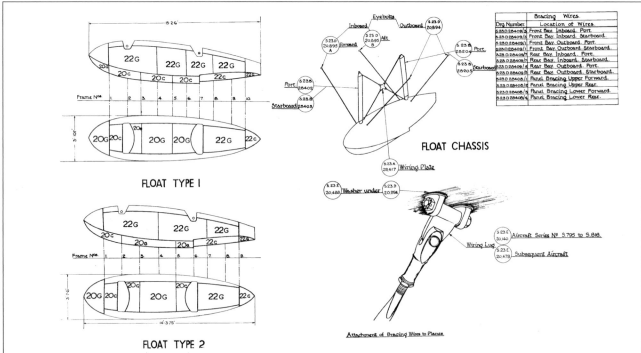

	Bracing Wires.
Drg Number.	Location of Wires.
S.23.D.28408/3	Front Bay. Inboard. Port.
S.23.D.28408/5	Front Bay. Inboard. Starboard.
S.23.D.28408/1	Front Bay. Outboard. Port.
S.23.D.28408/7	Front Bay. Outboard. Starboard.
S.23.D.28408/4	Rear Bay. Inboard. Port.
S.23.D.28408/6	Rear Bay. Inboard. Starboard.
S.23.D.28408/2	Rear Bay. Outboard. Port.
S.23.D.28408/8	Rear Bay. Outboard. Starboard.
S.23.D.28408/1	Panel Bracing Upper Forward.
S.23.D.28408/8	Panel Bracing Upper Rear.
S.23.D.28408/9	Panel Bracing Lower Forward.
S.23.D.28408/4	Panel Bracing Lower Rear.

FLOAT TYPE 1

FLOAT TYPE 2

FLOAT CHASSIS

down into the bilge. Each compartment between bulkheads had a drain plug in the bottom plating.

The cast light-alloy chassis attachment fittings were bolted in the float troughs at float Frame 2 (all types), Frame 7 for Type 1 or Frame 6 for Type 2. Stainless steel lugs on the chassis fittings allowed the wing bracing and panel bracing wires to be attached. The chassis consisted of two extruded light-alloy tubes, encased in folded light-alloy streamline casings. The ends of the casings were faired in with Celastoid plastic cuffs, which cracked when the 'boats were in service.

The floats were braced inboard and out with swaged steel wires, ending with eyebolts fitted to lugs on the bottom trusses of the spars. The bracing wires were prone to pull out of the swaged ends in service and they kept breaking in the air, so they were redesigned to be replaced with cables.

The floats were water-tested by filling alternate compartments to check for seepage. A steadying eye, for use during beaching operations, was attached to the aft end of some floats.

The 28 S.23 'boats with Type 2 floats were originally fitted with an ingenious patented sprung panel bracing, enclosed in a streamlined, transparent cellulose-acetate plastic housing. The mechanism proved unsatisfactory in service and was soon replaced with a much simpler, unsprung X-shaped wiring plate. The revised Type 2 float chassis was braced diagonally with longer crossed wires, held at the cross by an acorn assembly.

Electrical system

The main electrical switchboard was a Rotax N5 EX switchbox complete with the six main switches, the fuses, a voltmeter, and an ammeter. It was fixed on the starboard side of the control deck between the mail loading hatch and Frames 15/16. The battery was a 24-volt 18-cell Nife alkaline type with a capacity of 55 ampere hours, connected to the generators via two Rotax N5 FF voltage regulators on the main switchboard. The power for the electrical installation was supplied from the two 1,000-watt Rotax N2 BW 24-volt generators mounted as auxiliaries on the inner engines.

ABOVE Wing tip float showing the original sprung bracing.
(Shorts)

The battery supplied:

■ **24-volt circuits**
Navigation lights
Searchlights for alighting
Power supply for radio installation
Internal lighting
Steward's call signals
Flap motor

■ **12-volt circuits**
Instrument lighting
Engine starting for emergency use when ground battery was not available

LEFT Electrical panel.
(Shorts)

The Desiderio Type 500 screw-action emergency starting switch (usually known as the Dizzy) was on the 12-volt circuit to the engine starter motors. The Dizzy had to be screwed fully in to bring it into operation, and screwed a full 1½ turns out to break the circuit. The Tucker B 70 two-way changeover switch connected the starter button circuit, either to the battery or the Niphan NFAB ground plug. Both this switch and the Dizzy were on the main switchboard.

The 'boats were fitted with searchlights for use during night operations. The bow searchlight, between Frames 1 and 2 on the port side, was an 8in-diameter 240-watt Smith-Harley unit on a retractable and adjustable mounting. The wing searchlight, in the leading edge of the starboard mainplane only, was a fixed 10in-diameter 500-watt Smith-Harley unit, mounted behind an acetate transparency in the leading edge, between mainplane Diaphrams 14 and 15, outboard of the outer engine. The searchlights (bow and wing) were energised by a three-position switch, mounted in the coupé on the port side of the aircraft. Moving the switch from the OFF position to the first ON position (F 1) brought the bow light in directly. Moving the switch to position F 2 completed the circuit to the wing light. Only one searchlight could be used at a time.

The navigation lights, red for the port side and green for starboard, were Rotax A5C/492 phenolic mouldings projecting from the leading edge of each half-mainplane, just inboard of the end of the spar. The navigation lights had an arc of visibility of 67° on either side of the aircraft's centre line, making a total sweep of 135°.

The Rotax K 625 identification light was located on the underside of the starboard mainplane, just forward of the forward spar truss, 13ft out from the root. A drift sight was fitted in the starboard mainplane root, accessible from the control deck.

Flying boats were considered to be surface vessels measuring under 150ft in length, so were required to carry a white anchor, or riding, light, a steaming light, and an overtaking light. The anchor light had to be visible all round for a distance of 2 miles, and the steaming light had to have a visibility, from the front of the aircraft, of 3 miles in an arc that extended 112° on either side, making a total of 225°. On the Empire 'boats both these lights were in a combined fitting at the top of the ensign mast, nested inside the aerial mast. The overtaking light acted as a tail light in the air.

The schedule of light fittings was as follows:

Mooring compartment	one	6-watt light
Control deck	two	6-watt roof lights
Mail room	three	6-watt roof lights
Receiving space	one	6-watt roof light
Loading space	one	6-watt roof light
Chart table	one	6-watt light
Stowage room	two	6-watt roof lights
Forward cabin	seven	6-watt wall and bunk lights
	two	36-watt ceiling lights (1 with 6-watt pilot)
Corridor	one	6-watt ceiling light
Lavatories	one	6-watt ceiling light each
Pantry	two	12-watt ceiling lights
Centre cabin	two	6-watt wall and bunk lights
	one	36-watt ceiling lights (1 with 6-watt pilot)
Promenade cabin	seven	6-watt wall and bunk lights
	three	36-watt ceiling lights (1 with 6-watt pilot)
Aft cabin	five	6-watt wall and bunk lights
	two	36-watt ceiling lights (1 with 6-watt pilot)
Freight room	one	6-watt ceiling light

The steward's call signal indicator was fitted to the wall of the pantry. There were different coloured indicator lights for each cabin: red for the forward cabin, white for the centre cabin, green for the promenade cabin, and amber for the aft cabin. There were nine call button positions in the forward cabin, seven in the centre cabin, nine in the promenade cabin, and seven in the aft cabin. The later 'boats also had a call button on the control deck.

Paintwork

No coatings were applied to the external Alclad surfaces of the 'boats in Imperial Airways Limited livery, except lanolin. The registration lettering, in the style of the 1930 Convention relating to the Regulation of Aerial Navigation was 7ft high for the upper and lower

LEFT Mk III S.30 long-range 'boat G-AFCU, *Cabot*, displaying the Imperial Airways hull markings. *(Shorts)*

BELOW G-ADHL, *Canopus*, in the wartime livery of BOAC, lands on Lagos Lagoon, Nigeria, for moorings at the Iquoi flying boat base. *(Imperial War Museum CH14753)*

ABOVE Tasman Empire Airways' S.30, ZK-AMC, was originally launched as ZK-AMA, *Ao-Tea-Roa*, but was re-registered ZK-AMC and renamed *Awarua*. *(British Airways Speedbird Heritage Centre)*

RIGHT *Clare* displays her wartime camouflage scheme at New York.

BELOW QANTAS Empire Airways' S.23, VH-ABB, *Coolangatta*, was impressed into the Royal Australian Air Force as A18-13. *(Author's collection)*

surfaces of the mainplanes and 3ft 6in high on either side of the hull. The aircraft's name was applied, in capitals, 12in high on either side of the nose, immediately below the windscreen side panels. The Maximum Permissible and Tare weights, 40,500lb and 27,000lb respectively for a standard S.23, were painted on the hull in 3in-high lettering below the starboard tailplane.

The livery was completed with the W/T bonding symbol stencilled on the movable flight surfaces and on the corresponding adjacent fixed surfaces on the aircraft. The operator's name and the aircraft's port of registry were added to the hull on both sides. The size and location of the lettering differed quite widely, but for the majority of 'boats it was in 10in-high capitals reading 'IMPERIAL AIRWAYS LONDON' or 'QANTAS EMPIRE AIRWAYS BRISBANE' low down on the hull between Frames 10 and 15. The TEAL 'boats were lettered 'TASMAN EMPIRE AIRWAYS WELLINGTON'. The S.23 'Atlantic' 'boats were lettered 'IMPERIAL AIRWAYS (ATLANTIC) LTD' high up on the hull. The style of the lettering was unique to the Empire 'boats. There is considerable variation in the position and height of the lettering on individual aircraft.

The colour of the lettering is controversial. For the IAL Empire 'boats the majority opinion is that it was dark blue, although it is difficult to see how a special colour could be maintained in service. The minority opinion is that it was black. After the incorporation of Imperial Airways into the British Overseas Airways Corporation, the original operator's name and port of registration was stripped from the hull. The Speedbird logo was added to most of the aircraft beneath the name, and the words 'BRITISH AIRWAYS', in 6in-high lettering.

The Second World War brought the underlining of the registration lettering on the hull and mainplanes with red, white, and blue bands, 12in wide. Fin or rudder flashes were added of varying lengths and in varying positions, but most being 3ft 6in high. Some of the 'boats were put into full camouflage with the registration lettering outlined in white. The last two S.33 'boats, *Clifton* and *Cleopatra*, were delivered in camouflage. The TEAL 'A' 'boats were not camouflaged but had the upper surface of the outer mainplane panels painted orange and carried union flags 2ft 6in by 5ft,

painted high up between Frames 6 and 8 on both sides of the hull.

The S.23M and the impressed 'boats, both British and Australian, were also fully camouflaged. Little evidence exists, but it is thought that the schemes complied with Air Ministry 'Order A 926/40 Coastal Command Temperate Sea Scheme', with the upper surfaces and hull finished in Pattern 1 format in 'extra dark sea grey' and 'dark slate grey' with Sky Type 'S' 'duck egg blue' undersurfaces. National 1 roundels (equal red and blue) 7ft in diameter were applied to the upper surfaces of the mainplanes, and National 3 (red, white, blue, and yellow) roundels 4ft 6in in diameter on the hull. No markings were carried on the under surfaces of the mainplanes. Three-colour fin flashes, 27in high by 24in wide, and serial numbers 'B' in 'light slate grey' completed the scheme. One of the few photos of the 'boats in colour shows *Clare* tied up to the pontoon in the USA, and a painting of AX659 *Clio* in camouflage is shown on the inside back cover of *Profile Publication No 84.*

The 'boats detached from the Horseshoe Route to evacuate British personnel from Crete were roughly and hurriedly camouflaged as they were moored on the Nile, with the hull down to the waterline.

Because of confusion with the markings of Japanese aircraft, the red centre of the roundel was omitted in later Australian service. A-18 *Clifton* had 'dull blue' and white roundels and fin flashes.

The fabric surfaces of the elevators and rudder were finished with dope to tighten and preserve them. A typical doping system to conform to DTD 83 consisted of a brush-applied first coat of red oxide dope, then the frayed edge-strips applied with clear dope as adhesive, then a second sun-resistant coat, followed by two pigmented silver finishing coats in the case of the pre-war Empire 'boats.

Cabin trimming

The interior trimming of the passenger cabins was designed by architect Brian O'Rorke ARIBA, and subcontracted to L.A. Rumbold & Co. Ltd. No reliable evidence exists as to the exact colours. The walls and ceilings of the

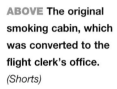

passenger cabins were finished in Connolly Bros Vaumol hide (fine leather), described variously as 'bottle green' or 'dark restful green' in colour. Carpets are described as 'grey' or, in some descriptions, 'mottled green and black'. Ceilings are described as 'white' for the forward cabin, and 'dove grey' or 'very pale lime green' for the other passenger cabins. The corridor between the pantry and the lavatories was finished in white paint for walls and ceiling. Trimming was completed with the fixing of the 'NO SMOKING' signs over the heads of the appropriate internal cabin doors, the square clock and matching altimeter in the centre cabin, the small holdalls let into the walls, the light luggage racks (light-alloy tube frame with netting stretched between, suspended from the ceiling with leather straps), the draw curtains at the windows, and the blinds at the ports.

The original specification called for 24 passenger seats. With this complement, the Mk I and Mk II S.23 'boats were fitted with a total of 17 adjustable seats in the centre, promenade, and aft cabins, and seven fixed seats in the forward cabin. When the forward cabin of the Mk I 'boats was taken over for the flight clerk's office, the passenger seating was reduced to the 17 adjustable seats, three in the centre cabin, eight in the promenade cabin, and six in the aft cabin.

The seats in the cabins were supplied to

Short Bros by IAL as embodiment loan or 'free issue' items. IAL was very proud of its new seats, and by contemporary standards they were considered to be extremely comfortable. The seat framework was fabricated from light-gauge electron tubing, and the assembly was licensed to Accles and Pollock Ltd in Birmingham. Each complete seat weighed 21lb. The seats had five positions, from the upright to the virtual recline. As the seat was moved downwards, a rubber cord on either side was put in progressive tension, to help move the seat back to a more upright position. The seat cushions and backs were Mosely 'Float-on Air' pneumatic cushions, covered in green, all-wool, uncut moquette with piped edges. The padded head and armrests were provided with detachable, washable covers. Bunk curtains

ABOVE The original smoking cabin, which was converted to the flight clerk's office. *(Shorts)*

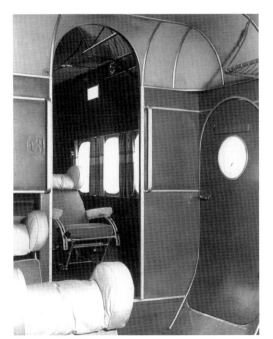

FAR LEFT The aft entry hatch on the port side with a view through to the aft cabin. When the original smoking cabin was converted for the flight clerk's office, this cabin became the no smoking cabin. *(Shorts)*

LEFT The promenade cabin looking forward, showing the centre cabin, the entry to the pantry and the smoking cabin beyond. *(Shorts)*

and coverlets were green to match the seat covering. The seat cushions doubled in duty as life preservers in the event of a ditching. Life rafts were not part of the equipment for the EAMP 'boats, but various references suggest life rafts were carried under wartime conditions, although no details have survived.

It was originally intended that the EAMP should be flown by day and night, so accommodation for 16 bunks was provided in the passenger cabins. Passenger seats folded down to a height of 15in, allowing the bunks to be rigged over them. The bunk frames, mattresses, pillows, sheets, and blankets were stowed in the space over the promenade cabin, accessible from the aft cabin. The bunk frames were designed with bolts at either end to fit into recesses in the walls of the cabins, spanning between the bulkheads or between a vertical pillar and a bulkhead. Tolerances were tight, and while it was possible to mount the bunks when the aircraft was on the water, trying the same operation in the air was another matter. The airframe flexed to a considerable degree in the air, especially in rough weather. It proved to be practically impossible to assemble the bunks in an acceptable time in flight, even with the flight clerk and steward working together. Other operational considerations also precluded

night flying on the EAMP, except in exceptional circumstances to make up lost time, so the idea of passengers sleeping on board the 'boats while on normal service was abandoned. The bunks were brought back on the wartime Horseshoe Route 'boats, but for seating rather than sleeping.

Pyrene fire extinguishers were located on both decks:

- **Upper deck**
  Starboard side near deck at Frame 7
  Starboard side on roof between Frames 13 and 14
- **Lower deck**
  Forward cabin on left-hand side of entry hatch
  Pantry on right-hand side of ladder to upper deck
  Promenade cabin on left-hand side of entry from corridor and on left-hand side of bulkhead at entry to aft cabin
  Aft cabin on right-hand side of entry from promenade cabin

Radios

The radio installations provided to IAL were on lease from Marconi's Wireless Telegraph Co. Ltd. Hermes radios were fitted to some of the later aircraft.

BELOW Wireless equipment. *(Shorts)*

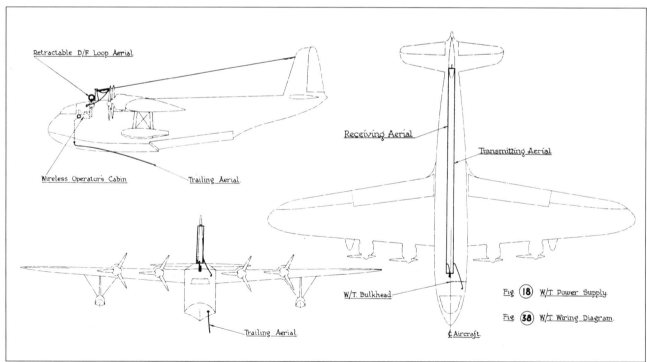

Normal range Mk I S.23 'boats' 1937 equipment:

Transmitter	AD 57A (HD 1011) short wave AD 57A (HD 1012) medium wave
Receiver	AD 5782 A (HD 1016) short wave and medium wave
Anode converter	(HD 1005)
Visual D/F attachment	Type 626C (HD 1032)
Aerial switch and earthing relay	Type 190 (HD 1044)
Charging switchboard	Type H 230A (HD 1041)
Fixed dipole aerial (on early aircraft only)	
Fixed aerial replaced by dual aerial with spreaders	
D/F loop	
Double pole on–off switch	

Mk II S.23 'boats, *Centaurus* and *Cavalier,* had extra equipment for the survey flight to Australasia and for the North American service. For the North American service a radio-telephone set, AD 37K medium- and long-range R/T was fitted.

Long-range Mk III S.23 Atlantic 'boats' 1937 equipment – *Caledonia* and *Cambria*:

Transmitter	AD 73A (HD 1011) short wave A.1 wave AD 73A (HD 1017) medium wave A.2 wave
Receiver	AD 5872 B (HD 1019)
Stand-by receiver	AD 5062B (HD 1007) medium-wave D/F in USA
Anode converter	(HD 1009)
Barrater unit filament heater	(HD 1030)
Visual D/F attachment	Type 626B (HD 1023)
D/F reversing hand switch	(HD 1010)
Earthing relay	Type 190 (HD 1044)
Charging switchboard	Type H 230A (HD 1041)
Fixed dual aerial with spreaders	
Aerial switch	
D/F loop	
Double pole on–off switch	

For North American service an AD 37K medium- and long-range R/T radio-telephone set was fitted.

Normal range 'boats' 1938 equipment used on S.30 and S.33 'boats, except for the four Mk III long-range 'boats:

Transmitter	AD 67A Ed. A (HD 1083) short and medium wave
Receiver	AD 6872B Ed. H (HD 1138)
Transceiver (S.30 'boats)	Hermes 1050A/1051A D/F
ML converter	Type C (modified)
D/F reversing hand switch	Type 180A (HD 1010)
Voltage control unit	Type 580A
Aerial switch	Type H 130B
Charging switchboard	Type H 230A (HD 1041)
D/F loop	Type 823/18
On–off switch	Type H 240A Fixed aerial
Fixed aerial	

Alternative 1938 equipment used on the four S.30 Mk III long-range 'boats, *Cabot*, *Caribou*, *Connemara*, and *Clyde*:

Transmitter	AD 67A Ed. A (HD 1083) short and medium wave
Receiver	AD 6872B Ed. H (HD 1138)
D/F receiver	AD 5062E Ed. H (HD 1145)
Telephone ML converter	Type C (modified)
ML converter	Type C (with relay)
D/F reversing hand switch	Type 180A (HD 1010)
Voltage control unit	Type 580A
Aerial switch	Type H 130B (spec)
Charging switchboard	Type H 230A (HD 1041)
Fixed dual aerial	
D/F loop	Type 823/18
On–off switch	Type 240A

The direction-finding aerial (D/F) on the S.23 Mk I 'boats was a retractable 13in-diameter circular, rotatable, screened loop aerial linked to the receiver. The whole apparatus was arranged to slide vertically upwards on the two guide tubes from the body of the aircraft and into the airstream clear of the screening effects of the metal hull. The later S.30 and S.33 aircraft, and some of the S.23 'boats, on the Horseshoe Route were fitted with non-retractable 18in-diameter loops.

The fixed aerial was a double longitudinal T aerial, fitted with spreaders at both ends. The port aerial was for transmission and the starboard for reception.

The trailing aerial winch was on the port side of the aircraft, behind the captain's seat. The aerial was a 280ft phosphor bronze wire, wound on to the storage drum of a hand-operated winch. The wire ended with a string of lead weights to prevent it from whipping about in the air. With the winch lever to 'free', the aerial was run out, under the control of a centrifugal brake. To wind in, the lever was set to 'fixed' and the aerial was wound in by hand against a ratchet mechanism. The aerial wire left the aircraft through a retractable Paxolin fairlead. In the 'down' position, the fairlead projected 24in vertically downwards, clear of the planing bottom on the port side just aft of Frame 6. In the 'up' position, the aperture was closed off by a watertight rubber flap.

Power for the radio equipment ran in screened cables from the generators on the inner engines to the motor generator set. The power for the transmitter was supplied by the motor generator set, which was switched on through the generator-charging switchboard each time a transmission was made.

A motor generator set was provided for emergency use on the water. The set, in its 'fireproof container', consisted of a Stanley Type SM 5M 1hp two-stroke petrol engine (driving the 24-volt FB/M1 electric motor that was normally powered by the aircraft's electrical system) and a Type FB/G1 double output generator, all coupled together. In normal conditions on the water and in flight,

the FB/G1 generator was powered by the electric motor. The generator supplied HT power at 1,200-volt, 200-milliamp DC, and LT power at 12.5-volt, 6-amp DC. If the petrol engine was required for use, the 'fireproof container' was opened up and the exhaust pipe fitted, leading to the outside of the aircraft through the direct vision panel of the windscreen on the captain's side. Very noisy in operation, the set provided enough power for effective communication. The fuel tank was drained after each operation. It was also possible for the petrol motor to charge the aircraft's battery. The 'fireproof container' was situated on the control deck between the captain's seat and the radio officer's station.

Engines – Pegasus and Perseus

The year 1932 was an eventful one in the prehistory of the Empire 'boats, for in that year the Bristol Aeroplane Company Ltd published details of their two new engines, the Pegasus with poppet valves (a direct development of Bristol's Jupiter engine) and the Perseus with sleeve valves – both nine-cylinder, geared, air-cooled radials. The use of air-cooled engines for the Empire 'boats was an IAL requirement, following their successful use of the Bristol Jupiter engines on the Calcutta and Kent flying boats, and the L.17 Scylla landplanes. Both the Bristol Pegasus and the Perseus radial engines were fitted to the Empire 'boats – Pegasus to all marks of the S.23s, the S.33 'boats, and the first and last of the S.30 aircraft, *Champion* and *Cathay*, and Perseus to the other seven S.30 'boats. Both types of engine were geared down through Farman-type epicyclic reduction gearing to turn the airscrew at half crankshaft speed.

The engine nacelles of the 'boats were designed to accommodate either engine without modification. The engines were supplied to Short Bros by the Bristol Aeroplane Company as embodiment loan or 'free issue' items. They were delivered complete with carburettors and starter motors, bonded and screened to DTD GEL 125 – 'Bonding of the Ignition System' – up to the starting magneto and the primary short-

BELOW The starboard inner Pegasus engine of *Canopus* fixed in position on the nacelle, complete with collector ring and gills but without cowling or exhaust pipe. *(Shorts)*

PEGASUS XC

The Pegasus XC was a 28.7-litre, civil-rated, medium-supercharged, poppet-valved, nine-cylinder radial engine:

Bore	5.75in
Stroke	7.50in
Capacity	28.7 litre
Airscrew rotation	LH tractor
Compression ratio	6.75:1
Overall diameter	55.3in
Net dry weight	1,030lb

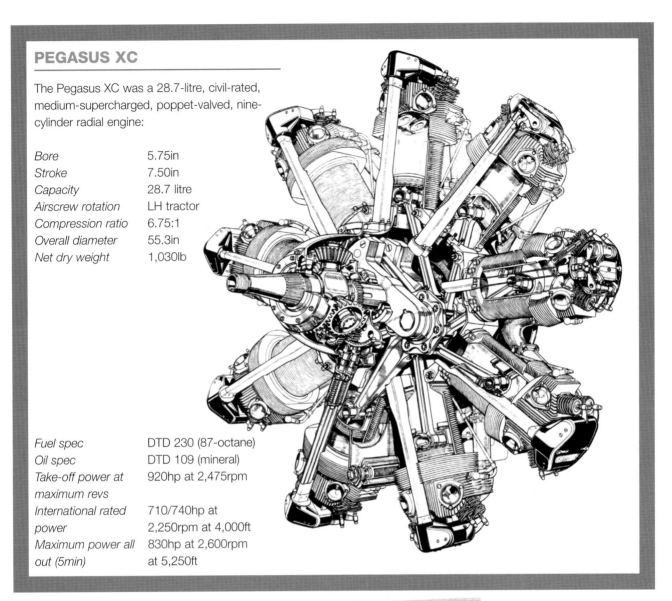

Fuel spec	DTD 230 (87-octane)
Oil spec	DTD 109 (mineral)
Take-off power at maximum revs	920hp at 2,475rpm
International rated power	710/740hp at 2,250rpm at 4,000ft
Maximum power all out (5min)	830hp at 2,600rpm at 5,250ft

circuiting terminals of the main magnetos. The fitting of the engines, the exhaust collector rings, inter-cylinder cooling baffles, NACA long chord cowlings with attached cooling gills, and the supply and fitting of the Record engine speed indicators, Marconi screened ignition harnesses, and the auxiliaries was the responsibility of Short Bros. The airscrews were supplied and fitted by Short Bros. The IAL order of 136 Pegasus XC engines was considered a big one in 1935. The Pegasus developed into a highly successful engine with a run approaching 32,000 of all types before production finally ceased.

Pegasus XXII engines were fitted to the two S.33 'boats. When they became more plentiful during the Second World War, the

ABOVE The nine-cylinder, single-row, air-cooled Bristol Pegasus radial engine was first introduced in 1932. It was used to power the Empire 'boats as well as enjoying widespread use during the Second World War in the Harrow, Wellington, Hampden, Vildebeest, Swordfish and Sunderland.
(Author's collection)

LEFT The manufacturer's engine plate was displayed prominently in the cockpit.

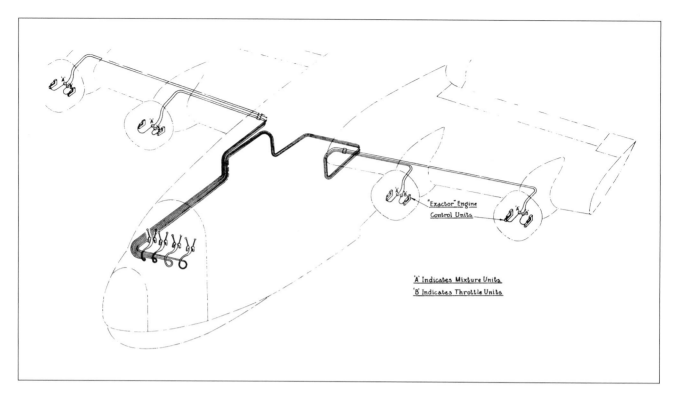

ABOVE **Engine controls.** (Shorts)

'A' Indicates Mixture Units.
'B' Indicates Throttle Units.

more powerful Pegasus XXII was fitted in exchange for the Pegasus XC engines to some of the S.23s during major overhauls. The XXII engines, running on 100-octane-rated spirit, were identical to the XCs with the exception of the supercharger, which had an 11in-diameter rather than the 9½in-diameter impeller of the XCs. The preferred spark plugs, two plugs per cylinder, were 14mm-diameter KLG RV 7/5 or RV 7/4. During the Second World War, Lodge RS 14/2R and Sphinx R2 14R plugs were sometimes substituted.

The Mk XII C version of the Perseus engine, used to power seven of the S.30 'boats developed 890hp maximum take-off power, about 4% less than the Pegasus XC. The Perseus also had a slightly smaller overall diameter than the Pegasus, with 6% less frontal area. Perseus engines had two 14mm spark plugs per cylinder, specially made by KLG with an extended metal sleeve to protect the body of the plug in the junkhead of the cylinder.

The magnetos fitted to both types of engines, two per engine, were dual Rotax-Watford SP 9-6 magnetos with screened distributors, mounted on the rear casings for the Pegasus and off the auxiliary drive for the Perseus engines, driven by the crankshaft at 9/8 of engine speed. Both types of engine were fitted with Claudel Hobson Duplex type ATV 85E carburettors.

The engine auxiliaries were driven off the tailshaft, their arrangement depending on the type of engine and automatic pilot fitted to the aircraft. For the Pegasus engines the auxiliaries were mounted on the backplate, while the Perseus engines had a flexible drive to a gearbox that drove all the auxiliaries, enabling them to be left in place when an engine was changed. The electrical generators were

PERSEUS XII C

Bristol Perseus XII C was a 24.9-litre civil-rated, medium-supercharged, nine-cylinder, sleeve-valve engine:

Bore	5.75in
Stroke	6.50in
Capacity	24.9 litre
Airscrew rotation	LH tractor
Compression ratio	6.54:1
Overall diameter	51.8in
Net dry weight	1,070lb
Fuel spec	DTD 230 (87-octane)
Oil spec	DTD 109 (mineral)
Take-off power at maximum revs	890hp at 2,700rpm
International rated power	680/710hp at 2,250rpm at 4,000ft
Maximum power all out (5min)	815hp at 2,600rpm at 6,000ft

common to both types, but the number and location of vacuum pumps, air compressors, and oil pumps differed.

The auxiliaries on the Pegasus XC engines and Pegasus XII C engines for the S.23, S.30 and S.33 aircraft with Sperry automatic pilot were arranged as follows:

Port inner engine	Sperry-Northern PL1335 oil pump Rotax Type N2.BW electrical generator
Starboard inner engine	Turner-Romec rotary-vane pump, with relief valve incorporated Rotax Type N2.BW electrical generator
Starboard outer engine	Romec vacuum pump

The auxiliaries on the gearboxes of the three

S.30 'A' aircraft with Perseus XII C engines and Smith automatic pilot were as follows:

Port inner engine	RAE Type C air compressor complete with its own oil system and cooler
Starboard inner engine	Romec vacuum pump Rotax Type N2.BW electrical generator

Engine lubrication for both engines was by the dry sump principle. The pressure pump fed oil to the master connecting rod, the big-end bearings, cam gear, rear cover, and reduction gears. The remainder of the moving parts of the engine were lubricated by splash from the sump at the bottom of the crankcase, between cylinder Nos 5 and 6. The oil was returned from the sump to the oil tank by the scavenge pump via the carburettor jacket, the oil filter, and oil cooler.

BELOW Shorts' fitters give their attention to the starboard outer Pegasus of *Canopus* on the slipway at Rochester. Note the open maintenance platforms. *(British Airways Speedbird Heritage Centre)*

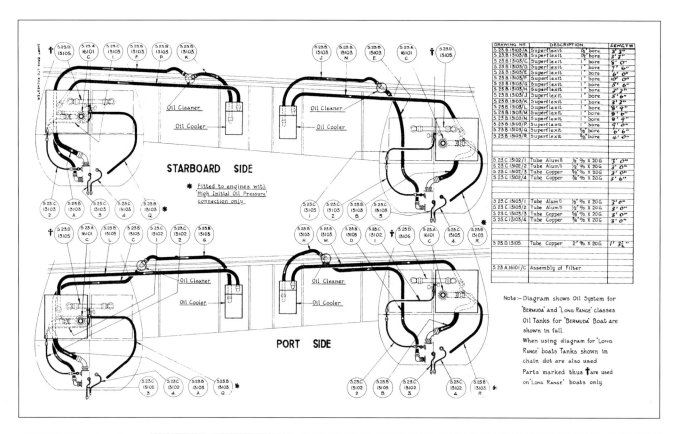

DRAWING Nº	DESCRIPTION		LENGTH
S.23.B.13103/A	Superflexit	1½" bore	3' 2"
S.23.B.13103/B	Superflexit	1½" bore	3' 2"
S.23.B.13103/C	Superflexit	1" bore	7' 6"
S.23.B.13103/D	Superflexit	1" bore	7' 6"
S.23.B.13103/E	Superflexit	1" bore	6' 0"
S.23.B.13103/F	Superflexit	1" bore	10' 0"
S.23.B.13103/G	Superflexit	1" bore	5' 6"
S.23.B.13103/H	Superflexit	1" bore	3' 2½"
S.23.B.13103/J	Superflexit	1" bore	5' 6"
S.23.B.13103/K	Superflexit	1" bore	3' 9"
S.23.B.13103/L	Superflexit	1" bore	3' 9"
S.23.B.13103/M	Superflexit	1" bore	9' 9"
S.23.B.13103/N	Superflexit	1" bore	8' 9"
S.23.B.13103/P	Superflexit	1" bore	9' 0"
S.23.B.13103/Q	Superflexit	⅝" bore	6' 6"
S.23.B.13103/R	Superflexit	⅝" bore	4' 0"
S.23.C.13102/1	Tube Alumⁿ	½"ø x 20G	3' 0"
S.23.C.13102/2	Tube Alumⁿ	½"ø x 20G	3' 0"
S.23.C.13102/3	Tube Copper	⅝"ø x 20G	3' 0"
S.23.C.13102/4	Tube Copper	¾"ø x 20G	3' 6"
S.23.C.13103/1	Tube Alumⁿ	½"ø x 20G	3' 0"
S.23.C.13103/2	Tube Alumⁿ	½"ø x 20G	3' 0"
S.23.C.13103/3	Tube Copper	⅝"ø x 20G	3' 0"
S.23.C.13103/4	Tube Copper	¾"ø x 20G	3' 0"
S.23.D.13105	Tube Copper	2"ø x 20G	1' 3½"
S.23.A.16101/C	Assembly of Filter		

STARBOARD SIDE

Oil Cleaner

Oil Cooler

* Fitted to engines with 'High Initial Oil Pressure' connection only.

PORT SIDE

Oil Cleaner

Oil Cooler

Note:- Diagram shows Oil System for 'BERMUDA' and 'LONG RANGE' classes. Oil Tanks for 'BERMUDA' Boat are shown in full.
When using diagram for 'LONG RANGE' boats Tanks shown in chain dot are also used.
Parts marked thus † are used on 'LONG RANGE' boats only.

ABOVE Oil system for Bermuda and long-range classes. *(Shorts)*

RIGHT Engine oil leaks were not uncommon on the Empire 'boats. Here a fitter cleans oil slicks from the upper mainplane of *Caledonia*. Note the line and harness attached to his waist as a safety precaution. *(British Airways Speedbird Heritage Centre)*

The exhaust gases were taken forward from the cylinders to a collector ring, or exhaust manifold, on the leading edge of the cowling, built up from riveted sheet steel. The cowling was fixed on the engine nacelle with a three-point rubber anti-vibration mounting. The exhaust pipe was 6in in diameter and taken from the manifold between Nos 3 and 4 cylinders, through the leading edge of the mainplane in a steel duct with a 1in clear annular air space, to discharge over the upper surface of the mainplane. The exhaust pipe of the starboard inner engine was fitted with a muff-type water boiler for the aircraft's heating system. The exhaust pipes originally ended flush with the top surface of the mainplane. The Type Certificate of Airworthiness mentioned that exhaust gases impinging 'on the stressed metal covering of the upper surface of the main planes might in time effect the characteristics of the metal'. Extension stubs were fitted to divert the exhaust gases safely away.

Engines were delivered to No 3 Shop by road from Bristol, off-loaded, slung, and transferred by crane across the shop to the Engine-fitting Shop for preparation. Prepared engines were transferred back across the shop to their final fixing position on the mainplane. The net dry weight of a Pegasus XC engine on the sling was 1,081lb, with the Perseus XX engine slightly heavier. The cooling gill ring was placed round the nacelle before the engine was offered up for fixing. Still on the sling, the engine was positioned so that the nine ⅜in-diameter fixing bolts could be inserted through the mounting holes in the nacelle mounting ring, and be tightened up. The engine was bonded to the nacelle. The cooling gill ring was then brought forward and fixed. The gills were opened and closed by a light roller chain that ran round the circumference of the ring, engaging in a sprocket at each gill plate. The whole mechanism was driven by another sprocket attached to a system of torque tubes and worm-drive gearboxes, ending with a flexible drive to gearboxes and operating handles in the wing roots. To save maintenance during wartime conditions, the adjusting mechanism and gills on some 'boats were removed altogether, and on others the cowling was modified to the equivalent of ⅓ open gills.

The flow of cooling air through the engine was controlled by adjustable gills attached to the aft edge of the cowling – adjustable between 0° and 30°. The cowlings of possibly all the Perseus-engined S.30 'boats were fitted with a reverse flow cooling arrangement. A five-part pressed sheet aluminium shroud was fitted round the collector ring so that the cooling air entered at the back, inside the cowling. The shroud funnelled the cooling air round the back of the collector ring and discharged it forwards, over the outside of the ring. The more efficient cooling of the exhaust system more than compensated for the extra drag and weight.

The airscrews fitted initially to all the 'boats were de Havilland 5000 series, two-position, variable pitch units of 12ft 9in diameter. The prepared and balanced airscrews, each weighing 365lb, were slung and brought to their respective engine by crane. The airscrews were offered up to the splined engine shaft, coated with anti-seizing compound, slid on to the shaft, and the airscrew piston screwed up and the split pins inserted in the piston locking ring. The cylinder cover was then screwed on and the sling removed. The Perseus-engined 'boats were equipped with constant speed units. By 1943, the two TEAL 'A' flying boats had been fitted with fully-feathering de Havilland Hydromatic constant speed airscrews – the only Empire 'boats to be so equipped. The airscrews were supplied and installed by Short Bros.

The Perseus engines of *Cabot* and *Caribou* were fitted with Graviner fire-suppression equipment. Each engine was fitted with a red-banded copper bottle, filled with 2.72kg of methyl bromide, charged with nitrogen under pressure of 60psi. Operation was by a push button, a flame switch set at 60°C, or an inertia switch that operated instantly at not less than 6g. When actuated, an electrically operated fuse in the head of the bottle opened the explosive discharge head, to empty the bottle in a few seconds. Distribution pipes ran from the discharge head to spray the engine surface, especially the exhaust manifold and pipes, and the inside of the cowling. Initially, oil from the Sperry oil supply tanks, mounted just above the bottles, leaked on to the discharge heads, rendering them useless. Orange-banded bottles with oil-resistant heads were substituted.

Chapter Six

Flying the 'C' class

A crew of five – captain, first officer, radio officer, flight clerk and steward – was required to operate an Empire 'boat, with the operating pilots needing additional skills in seamanship, especially where leaving harbour or taking up moorings was concerned. The passenger complement could vary between 16 and 24, depending on the route being flown.

OPPOSITE Palestine was one of the ports of call for Empire 'boats in the Middle East. Here, *Challenger* is refuelled at Tiberias on the Sea of Galilee. *(US Library of Congress)*

Flight crew

An EAMP crew consisted of the captain and first officer as the pilots, a radio officer, a flight clerk (later translated into purser) and, normally, one steward. The Bermuda–New York service was flown without a flight clerk and carried instead an assistant steward. On the Horseshoe Route, the steward was often dispensed with, as the standard of cuisine no longer required his skilled administration. On these services the flight clerk stood in for the steward when required. As conditions on the Horseshoe Route became more difficult, the service was flown without pursers or stewards.

Captains and First Officers

Captains held a current 'B' Licence, a First Class Navigator's Licence ('First N'), 'A' and 'C' Engineer's Licences, and (most of them) a Wireless Operator's Licence. Selected captains took a nine-month course in celestial navigation at IAL's school at Croydon in preparation for the transatlantic survey flights.

A first officer was required to be over 23 years of age, to hold a current 'B' Licence with more than 1,000 hours solo, to have more than 500 flying hours on twin-engined aircraft, experience of night flying, a Second Class Navigator's Licence ('Second N'), an 'A' Licence (authority to issue a Daily Flight Certificate for aircraft), a 'C' Licence (authority to issue a Daily Flight Certificate for the engines), and an 'X' Licence (covering the repair of instruments and magnetos).

WHY PASSENGERS PREFER IMPERIAL AIRWAYS

1 **BECAUSE** of its unrivalled experience

2 **BECAUSE** of the high standards of efficiency and comfort

3 **BECAUSE** its air liners are the most comfortable in the world

4 **BECAUSE** its latest air liners are equipped with four engines

One of the Captains of Imperial Airways. He is one of many who have spent over 10,000 hours in the air

TOP AND LEFT With his immaculate appearance and steely gaze, Captain O.P. Jones (front row, third from left) was the 'face' of Imperial Airways publicity in the 1930s – highly professional and dependable. *(US Library of Congress/Author)*

LEFT Imperial Airways gold bullion embroidered pilot's wings. *(Author's collection)*

Some first officers also had a Wireless Operator's Licence. The aircraft carried a tool kit enabling him to change spark plugs and engine cylinders, and other items, such as starter motor booster coils, if the need should arise – and it did at the start of operations. Captains and first officers had to pass a six-monthly medical to revalidate their 'B' Licences, and pass an instrument rating test.

On 29 June 1937, the Empire Air Mail Scheme became the Empire Air Mail Programme. A typical Empire Air Mail Programme service round trip to Singapore consisted of flying about 42 sectors in 115 flying hours in 18 days. Depending on the weather, this could involve some strenuous manual flying. Captains could expect a period of between eight to ten days before being rostered for the next service. The interval between trips was occupied in reporting at Hythe, possibly another one or two days' reporting in London, and the odd test flight after maintenance – and resting, as flying the EAMP could be physically demanding. As the service pay depended on the hours flown, captains' duties were rostered to share out the flying hours as equally as possible. The number of flying hours was controlled by law. Pilots of passenger-carrying aircraft were allowed to fly for a maximum of 125 hours in any 30-day period, a theoretical yearly total of 1,520 hours, compared to the current (1 May 1990) Civil Aviation Authority maxima of 100 hours per month and 900 hours per year.

Master Air Pilot's Certificates had been instituted in 1929 for pilots of civil aircraft. The requirements for this certificate were a current 'B' Licence, 1,000 hours as pilot of a civil aircraft during the preceding five years, 20 night flights over land or sea beginning and ending in the dark, and a 'Second N' (Second Class Navigator's Licence) held for five years. Eighteen Master Certificates had been issued by August 1936, all to IAL captains. Some of the senior captains had served in the Royal Flying Corps in the First World War.

Captains for the new Empire 'boats were recruited from the four existing Operating Divisions and posted to the newly formed No 5 Empire Division. Some captains had transferred from the Mediterranean where they had been flying the Short flying boats of No 2 Division. Others transferred from the Handley Page HP42s of Nos 1 and 2 Divisions and the Armstrong Whitworth Atalanta XVs of Nos 3 and 4 Divisions.

In 1935, IAL approached the Air Ministry to allow volunteers to transfer from the Royal Air Force. Some of the RAF pilots agreeing to transfer had already had flying boat experience operating Short Rangoon and Singapore III 'boats. Pilots who had transferred from the RAF were sent to the IAL 'school', near the London Terminal Airport at Croydon, to qualify for their 'A' and 'C' Licences and for the Wireless Operator's Licence. They emerged, some 12 to 15 months later as acting first officers.

The conversion courses took place at Hamble, conveniently placed across Southampton Water from the new IAL base at Hythe. The three-month course taught aspiring flying boat captains and first officers seamanship in a course of 17 lectures. This was followed by 12 hours, solo and dual, in one of the two Saunders-Roe Cutty Sark amphibians, finishing with 20 hours, solo and dual, in one of the Short Calcutta 'boats, G-AATZ, or the Short Rangoon, G-AEIM. Landlubbers, three or four at a time, were given a two-week course on practical seamanship on a 10-ton ketch,

BELOW Imperial Airways Empire 'boat crew. Commanded by Captain G.J. Powell, the crew are flying *Cambria* across North Atlantic on the Second Experimental Flight. From left to right: P.A. Woods, J.H.A. Lewis, Captain G.J. Powell and C.F. Elder, 28 July 1937. *(TopFoto)*

skippered by a retired sea captain. No weeding out took place, and some senior captains, bred as they were on land aircraft, never managed to acquire a full grasp of the essentials of maritime operations.

When the newly transferred pilots finally arrived at the controls of an Empire flying boat, they revealed differences in approach and alighting technique, depending on the previous aircraft to which they had been accustomed. The tendency of ex-HP42 pilots was to glide in to alight slowly, with very little engine and full flap. Turning on to the final approach was often made at low level, with consequent loss of height. Realising that the wing float on the inside of the turn was in danger, they tended to pull up sharply to level off, alighting tail down, splashing in heavily with the risk of porpoising. Ex-Atalanta crews tended to approach straight in at a flat gliding angle, with a small amount of engine and a modicum of flap. This resulted in a flat, fast alighting with the 'boat running out for a considerable distance on the water. The curved top of the dashboard on the Empire 'boats did not give a clear horizontal reference. Pilots converting to the Empire 'boats tended to make their approach and alighting with the wing on their side down, with a potentially high mortality rate for wing floats. This tendency was corrected by rigging a wire between the blind brackets on either side of the coupé, straight across the pilot's field of vision, to establish a clear horizontal reference.

After training, captains and first officers were posted to No 5 Division to fly the routes as supernumeraries under the supervision of selected captains. Captain F.J. Bailey (then a veteran of some 20 years on marine aircraft) was the first IAL captain to gain command of *Canopus* on 22 October 1936. In the early days of the Empire Air Mail Scheme, Captain Bailey or Air Superintendent Major Brackley checked out most captains before they were given command.

The first officer was second in command to the captain and was required to take command at any time should the captain become unable to act for any reason. He flew the aircraft as and when required and took on all the captain's responsibilities in his absence. He was accountable to the captain for the internal organisation of the aircraft, for the supervision of the duties of the other members of the crew, and for the aircraft being in a fit state to fly. At stations without a resident station engineer he would also be responsible for the daily check, including the engines, and would superintend the refuelling. On the flight-refuelled 'boats he acted as winchman.

During flight he was required to know the full details of the aircraft's position, its speed, fuel state, course, ETA, weather reports, air space restrictions, prohibited areas, and any warnings. The first officer was restricted to the same number of annual flying hours as a captain. On appointment with two licences, he was entitled to full basic pay and half service, or flying, pay. On obtaining his third licence he received full service pay. After three or four years as a first officer he might expect promotion to captain.

The particular route to be flown was decided by the captain after he had seen the weather forecast. He had absolute say as to whether he would make the flight if he considered the weather conditions were not to his liking at the point of take-off, over the sector, or at the destination. As the blind alighting aids then in use were considered impractical for flying boats, the weather conditions at the end of a flight were of vital importance. Alternative alighting areas were not readily available at many ports. Weather conditions also included the state of the water at the terminals, as the 'boats could operate in sea states that the attendant servicing vessels could not tolerate. In the case of sand and dust storms, the visibility at the alighting area decided whether a departure was made.

As instrument meteorological conditions hardly applied, most flying was done in visual flight rules. Most navigation with the short-sector distances was generally by dead reckoning. If the weather was clear, the sector between ports was flown by dead reckoning, with the position confirmed by known landmarks from a hand-held map. Drift could be checked with the drift sight in the starboard wing root of the 'boats. On sectors over oceans, position 'fixes' were obtained by sun, moon, and star sights by sextant. If the ground was obscured by cloud or when flying at night, the dead reckoning position was confirmed by radio direction-finding 'fixes' as necessary.

Radio officer

The radio officer's station on the Empire 'boats was on the port side of the control deck facing aft, literally back-to-back with the captain, so that communication between them could be immediate. The amount of traffic in wireless telegraphy (W/T), on an aircraft of the size of an Empire 'boat, required the full attention of the radio officer. When radio-telegraphy (R/T) was used, communications were still handled by him rather than directly by either pilot. After he had signed on and opened his station, the radio officer would be on watch for the duration of the flight. When he was not actually transmitting a message, he would be 'listening out' on the W/T international communications common calling frequency of 333kc/s (Hz), a continual period of concentration that started at take-off and lasted throughout the flight to just before alighting at the end. Before starting his watch at the radio sets, he had to attend to casting off the moorings, and to tying up before finishing at the end.

In 1936 the radio service was split into three broad divisions. The traffic division comprised point to point communications between aerodromes and included landlines and teleprinters as well as radio, the aircraft division included all communications between aircraft, and between aircraft and ground stations, including departure and position reports, special reports, and distress calls, and the third division covered the transmission of weather information, actual or forecast.

Most of the communication between the Empire 'boats and ground stations was by wireless telegraphy in the international Morse code. W/T was superior to radio telephony for long-range work and was less liable to interference. It also used a narrower bandwidth than R/T, a distinct advantage when all aviation radio traffic was squeezed into the 822- to 938-metre band. On the Empire routes over Africa and India, interference from intense sand and electrical storms, and from the monsoons, could blot out all medium-wave radio communication for hours. In these conditions short-wave W/T was the most reliable form of radio communication, as it was virtually free of atmospheric disturbance.

ABOVE The radio officer's station is on the right of the photo, showing the 1937 equipment for the normal range S.23 'boats. On the left of the photo, the control deck extends aft to the bulkhead at Frames 15/16. The escape hatch is open. The two ports on the starboard side are the mail loading hatch (rearmost) and over the navigator's chart table (folded down). *(Shorts)*

Three types of radio-wave form were in common use. Type A1 was the continuous, unmodulated, key-controlled form for use on the medium band for wireless telegraphy. Type A2 was a continuous-wave modulated, key-controlled form for use on the short-wave band, also known as interrupted continuous wave (ICW), and used for W/T. The Type A3 waves were of complex form and used for radio telephony.

The trailing aerial was normally used in the air and was best for long-distance work with the medium-wave sets. When a reasonable height had been gained after take-off, the radio officer extended the fairlead tube, set the lever to 'free' and allowed the trailing aerial to wind out. The aerials could then be switched from 'fixed' to 'trailing' by the changeover switch. With a trailing aerial, the range for R/T transmissions was between 250 and 300 miles and with the fixed aerial between 80 and 100 miles. All the various radio equipment carried by the Empire 'boats could receive and transmit R/T but it was not much used on the Empire routes.

The range of W/T transmission was impressive. Messages were received over distances of more than 3,250 nautical miles and up to 4,400 nautical miles on occasions. Working up to 2,000 nautical miles was not unusual, with 'boats in touch with each other in the air. Contacts were made by an Empire 'boat in the air over Southampton Water with ground stations at Alexandria and in India. Flying boats at Basra and Khartoum could be heard at Hythe. Communications from *Cavalier* on the inaugural flight from New York to Bermuda were heard in London. The broadcast of the coronation service of King George VI on 12 May 1937 was picked up by *Castor* and *Courtier* over the Mediterranean, and by *Cassiopeia* near Marseilles. The service was relayed to the passenger cabins. The reception was good.

The Q code was already in use by the shipping fraternity, and an aeronautical section was devised to cover aircraft operations. Commonly used messages, covering practically every eventuality, were assigned three-letter code groups, all starting with the letter Q. Each three-letter group had a specific meaning, which remained the same, irrespective of the languages spoken by either party to an

exchange. The group was either a statement or a question. The Q code speeded up radio traffic and neatly sidestepped the language problem at the same time. Although the code is now obsolete, vestiges remain in use today:

QAM Can you give me the latest meteorological weather report for …
QDM What is the magnetic course to steer, with zero wind, to reach you?
QFE Can you give me the present barometric pressure, not reduced to sea level, at the surface of … aerodrome
QFZ Can you give me a weather forecast for the region of …
QGH May I land using the procedure of descent through cloud?
QNH What is the barometric pressure at sea level?
QTE What is my true bearing in relation to …?

Ships used four-letter call signs, and aircraft used the five-letter group of their registration markings as their call sign. Given in full (but without the hyphen) at the start of an exchange of messages. They were normally abbreviated to a three-letter combination once communication was established. *Canopus*, registration G-ADHL, on making contact with a station for the first time, would call as 'GADHL'. Once contact had been made, the call sign could be shortened to 'G', plus the last two registration letters – 'GHL'. To avoid any possibility of confusion between three-letter aircraft call signs and those of ground stations, the Air Convention of 1930 required the registration authorities to proscribe certain letter groups in the registration of aircraft. Banned are any groups starting with the letter Q and such groups as SOS, PAN, TTT, XXX REF, and RPT.

Three direction-finding and position-fixing services were available to aircraft from ground stations. An aircraft could ask for a bearing from a single ground station by calling QTE – 'What is my true bearing in relation to you?' The ground station would respond with QTG – 'Will you send your call sign for 50 seconds followed by a dash of ten seconds on 377kc/s (frequency) in order that I may take your bearing?' If the bearing was, say 045°, the ground station would reply with 'QTE 045'.

LEFT On 5 July 1937 Empire 'boat *Caledonia,* commanded by Captain A.S. Wilcockson, flew from Foynes in the Irish Republic to Botwood, Newfoundland, thus becoming the first airliner to fly the North Atlantic in a westerly direction. The honours were shared with a Pan American Sikorsky flying boat, which crossed the Atlantic in the opposite direction at the same time. Because of adverse weather and 40mph headwinds, *Caledonia* flew much of the 1,200-mile journey only 1,000ft above the Atlantic. This photograph, taken on *Caledonia*'s return to Foynes after her epic flight, has been signed by her crew: Captain A.S. Wilcockson, Radio Officer T. Eric Hobbs and First Officer C.H. Bowes, and Radio Officer S.F. Mitchell. *(Author's collection)*

The second service was to give a position 'fix' from two or more ground stations. This was more accurate than from a single station, and it required three to get really reliable results. Ground stations that gave D/F bearings normally worked with two satellite stations that were alerted either by the control station by landline or radio, if they had not already heard the initial exchange, to take bearings on the aircraft and relay them back to the aircraft, either directly or through the control station. In normal conditions the 'QTE – QTG – QTE' procedure took up to a minute. A first-class bearing was accurate to 2°, so at a distance of 100 miles, the area of doubt was 12 square miles. A second-class bearing was accurate to 5°, and with a third-class bearing of more than 5°, the area of doubt increased to 300 square miles. Because of the time difference, when two or more stations were giving a position fix, the position lines did not close exactly when plotted on a chart. For a three-station fix the position lines enclosed a small triangular space – the area of doubt or 'the cocked hat' – with the

exact position of the aircraft being somewhere within the space.

The third service was to provide a course to steer to a ground station. The request from the aircraft was QDM – 'What is the magnetic course to steer, with zero, wind to reach you?' The reply from the ground station was the reciprocal of the magnetic bearing of the aircraft from the ground station, with no allowance for wind. In the final stages of an approach, QDMs could be given at the rate of four to six per minute, with the ground station serving one aircraft at a time. *Caledonia* was guided in to Botwood at the end of the

RIGHT Premier of the Irish Free State, Eamon De Valera, shakes hands with the commander of *Caledonia*, Captain Wilcockson, before the 'boat's departure for the USA. *(TopFoto)*

Foynes–Botwood sector of the first Atlantic flight on 6 July 1937. Captain A.S. Wilkcockson's log reads: 'At 09:40 to 09:55, I received a succession of QDMs and went to Botwood on them, arriving there at 10:02 GMT or two minutes behind my ETA.' Some ground control stations could also give aircraft a 'distance away' or a 'distance to go' as well as a bearing. Using its onboard D/F equipment, an aircraft could take its own bearings on known ground stations or radio beacons.

Flight clerk

Of the original 40 flight clerks at the start of the Empire Air Mail Scheme, 11 were 'converted' from IAL stewards working the Mediterranean flying boats and the Handley Page HP42s, two were transferred from the Traffic Department, and the rest recruited from outside the company. The positions were advertised in the press, asking for young men between the ages of 20 and 35, and 2,600 responded, including a bank manager, an ex-policeman, an ex-RAF pilot with 2,000 hours in his logbook, and some pursers already working on ocean-going ships.

The duties of this new crewmember were many and varied – 'boiler-suited jacks-of-all-trades' is how they described themselves. His prime responsibility was to deal with the increasingly formidable amount of paperwork associated with the Empire Air Mail Programme. He could attend to much of this work while the aircraft was airborne, and so reduce the time spent on the water at the many stops along the routes. One stop in 1938 was cleared in ten minutes, including the dropping and picking up of passengers, freight, and mail.

Trip times were the same as for the pilots. Flight clerks were rostered so that their earnings, dependent as they were on the days away from the UK, were approximately equal over the year. No overtime was paid.

In the early days, flight clerks learnt on their feet as they went, expediency and improvisation were the order of the day. A trainee would be supernumerary to an experienced flight clerk, and his tutor and the aircraft's captain would carefully watch his performance and potential. Two long flights were part of the training to assess the trainee's ability to cope with airsickness. A few of the experienced marine purser trainees found that the unpredictable motions of a flying boat, and the atmosphere of a somewhat temperamental heating and ventilating system, was too much for them.

The flight clerk prepared all the aircraft's 'papers' – the aircraft journey logbook, the daily certificate of safety, the 'snag sheet', the authorisation of operations of the wireless, the load sheet, the passenger list, manifests, bills of health, inoculation and vaccination cards, precious cargo transit check sheets (six copies of the consignment notes), mail waybills, passenger tickets, passports, the standard forms required at all ports, and the special forms required at some ports. Health, customs and immigration regulations and requirements changed so often that flight clerks needed to debrief at the Head Office in Victoria at the end of each service. He supervised and controlled the loading of all the 'dead load', bullion, diplomatic mail, letter and parcel mail, freight, company stores, and baggage for the passengers and crew, sometimes loading it himself (hence the boiler suit). He was personally accountable for over- or under-carries on his flights.

The freight and mail 'first off' was loaded into the aircraft 'last on'. The loading of the aircraft was his responsibility, including the calculation of the position of the aircraft's centre of gravity (CoG). The CoG calculation was done initially from the Short Bros' loading diagram, a long and tedious operation, calculating the lever arms fore and aft of the aircraft's datum point, and fraught with opportunities for unintentional error under pressure of time. The Traffic Department devised a loading slide rule, and some loading charts, which quickened the operation and reduced the possibilities of mistakes. When the slide rule became available it was normally used, with or without the loading charts in conjunction.

For a service, the flight clerk obtained from the Air and Catering Departments the names of the crew and the details of the mail, freight, and stores to be flown. A telephone call to the station superintendent at Hythe supplied him with details of the fuel and oil uplift. With this information, he was able to make a trial run of the load distribution. A passenger and baggage was taken to weigh 100kg – 75kg for the person and 25kg for the baggage. Passengers over 85kg in weight were limited to 15kg of baggage.

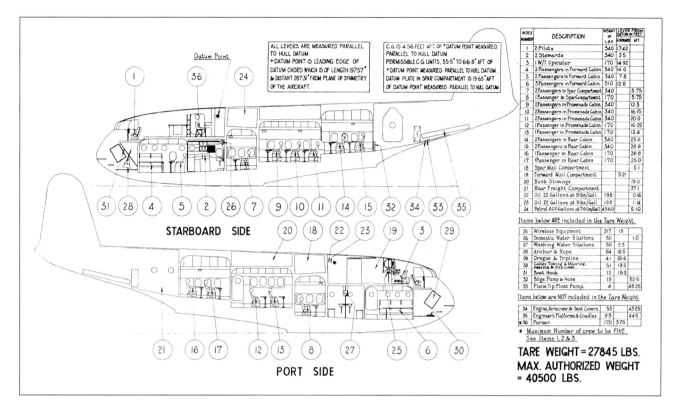

The flight clerk's original working station on the aircraft was at the aft end of the control deck, opposite the mail hatch on the starboard side and near the ladder to the escape hatch topside. When the 'boat was on the water, both these hatches were normally open, making it near impossible for him to carry on with his paperwork. When the 'boat was in the air, if a direct vision panel of the coupé was opened by one of the pilots, the strong forward-moving current of air could whip all his loose papers up in the air, to flutter down the length of the control deck and, occasionally, out through the open panel. Early in the EAMP operations, the forward passenger cabin on the lower deck was taken over as an office for the flight clerk and to stow additional mail and freight.

The flight clerk's kit comprised a lightweight Baby Empire portable typewriter, cleaned and complete with spare ribbon for each service, the 'papers' in his leather document case together with a loading slide rule and set of loading charts when available, an electric torch, a bullion locker padlock and key, a key for the hatches, a mail waybill book, a concertina folder for IAL mail, and a cash float and currency coupons. The currency coupons, valued at five shillings each, sold in books of ten at £2 11s 0d. They were used for small purchases during the flight and could be exchanged for local currency at IAL offices out of the UK. Flight clerks soon evolved a special technique of typing while in the air, to counteract the effects of bumpy weather – the Baby Empire was held down firmly on the desk with one hand, while typing with the other.

The flight clerk was responsible for crew and passengers' passports, publicity material, maps and guide booklets for night stops, timetables, stationery, currency coupons, quarantine forms, currency declarations, and aliens' cards. The Airmail Waybill Book kept track of the mail.

Many countries had restricted areas, and if the 'boats were flying anywhere near them, the passengers' cameras were impounded by the flight clerk and kept in a sealed camera box for the duration of that sector. He was also responsible for ensuring that the periodicals and newspapers were up to date and that the first-aid kit in the pantry was complete. Working with the steward, he was required to maintain the interior of the aircraft in a scrupulously clean condition, and, if needed, to help the steward with the preparation of meals and in attending to passengers' needs.

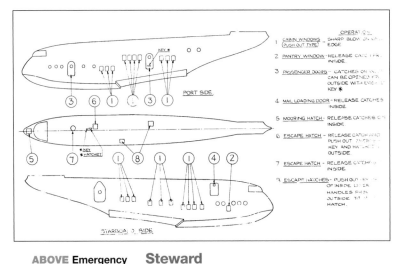

OPERATION

1 CABIN WINDOWS (PUSH OUT TYPE) – SHARP BLOW ON LOWER EDGE.

2 PANTRY WINDOW – RELEASE CATCH FROM INSIDE.

3 PASSENGER DOORS – CATCHES ON INSIDE. CAN BE OPENED FROM OUTSIDE WITH EMERGENCY KEY ✱.

4 MAIL LOADING DOOR – RELEASE CATCHES INSIDE.

5 MOORING HATCH – RELEASE CATCHES ON INSIDE.

6 ESCAPE HATCH – RELEASE CATCH AND PUSH OUT. EMERGENCY KEY AND HATCHET OUTSIDE.

7 ESCAPE HATCH – RELEASE CATCHES INSIDE.

8 ESCAPE HATCHES – PUSH OUT. ON INSIDE, USE HANDLES. FROM OUTSIDE, TRIP HATCH.

ABOVE Emergency escape measures. *(Shorts)*

Steward

Stewards were members of the Catering Department, and their prime responsibility was for the safety and comfort of passengers and the cleanliness of the passenger cabins. One steward looked after the full load of passengers, with the exception of the single-sector New York–Bermuda service on *Cavalier*. On this service, with a full complement of 24 passengers, an assistant steward was carried in place of the flight clerk.

Stewards were responsible for ordering the catering supplies and beverages for a flight, and for their reception and stowage in the pantry. Stores for a sector that included a meal could weigh 140kg loaded in hampers through the

inward-opening loading hatch above the pantry sink on the starboard side.

IAL claimed to be the first airline to offer 'restaurant'-quality meals in flight, considered to be of great importance for the passengers. Meals were prepared and cooked by high-quality caterers, and the cuisine offered was French, Italian, African, Indian, Malayan, and Netherlands East Indian, depending on the port of loading. All the hot and cold food and beverages were loaded in vacuum flasks and stowed for service in either the hot box or the ice chest as appropriate. Notwithstanding this, the range of catering offered on the peacetime services was impressive by any standard, and was considered by IAL to be better than that offered by the competition.

The total electrical generating capacity of a Mk I 'C' class 'boat did not allow for heating food, or for refrigeration. No cooking was done on the Empire 'boats. After stowing the consumable stores, the steward would check that the pantry water tank was full, that the first-aid kit and the emergency rations were in place in the pantry, and that the lights on the indicator board for the passengers' call system were all out. After take-off, he changed into his white patrol jacket before visiting the passenger cabins to distribute magazines, national daily newspapers, the aircraft's headed notepaper and picture postcards of the 'boat. On sectors when a meal

BELOW Smoking room and forward lounge. *(British Airways Speedbird Heritage Centre)*

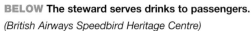

BELOW The steward serves drinks to passengers. *(British Airways Speedbird Heritage Centre)*

was served, he would wash and stow the cutlery and dishes before the 'boat alighted.

The flight clerk typed the menus – one for each passenger cabin. The steward took the menus through to the cabins and then saw to the needs of the crew. He returned to the passengers and took their orders, cabin by cabin. The pilot flying and the radio officer, unable to leave their working stations, had their meals brought to them by the steward, up the ladder from the pantry to the control deck. The flight clerk had his meal at his working station.

White linen tablecloths and serviettes, cutlery, side plates, and cruets for the number of covers were assembled on trays, taken through to the passenger cabins, and the tables laid up for the meal. Food was served on ceramic plates,

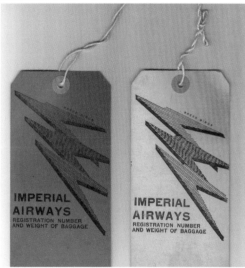

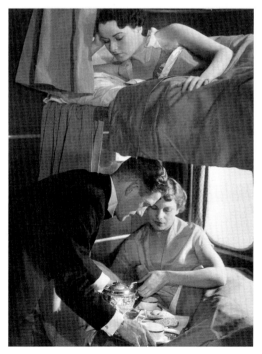

drinks were served in glasses, and cutlery was metal. OK and Worcester sauces, mayonnaise, and pickles were available. Doses of a mixture of chlorotone and caffeine were available to ward off airsickness.

The preparations in the pantry depended on the meal being served. Fruit was prepared first, fruit juices decanted from the vacuum flasks into serving jugs, and the bread rolls and Ryvita placed in baskets with preserves and butter on plates and covered with doilies. Hot food was served either from the hot box or from vacuum jars positioned ready for serving. The vacuum jugs for tea and coffee were positioned ready for use. Stewards soon mastered the

ABOVE The well-stocked pantry of Empire 'boat *Calpurnia. (British Airways Speedbird Heritage Centre)*

Typical menus in 1937 and 1938 were:

LUNCH
Challenger (date unknown)

Iced Melon
Roast Chicken, York Ham, Veal Galantine
Tomatoes and Asparagus Tips
Fresh Fruit Salad and Cream
Cheese – Cheshire, Cheddar, Cream Cheese
Toast Imperial Assorted Biscuits
Crystallised Fruit
Coffee and Liqueurs

DINNER
30 August 1938 (aircraft unknown)

Grapefruit or Consommé Princess
Roast Pheasant and Watercress
Lamb Cutlets and Mint Sauce
Roast Chicken, York Ham
Green Salad Beetroot and Apple Salad
Fresh Fruit Salad and Cream
Cheese – Cheddar, Gorganzola, Gruyère
Toast Imperial Assorted Biscuits
Coffee

DINNER
Corsair (date unknown)

Pâté de Fois Gras or Grapefruit
Roast Chicken, Ox Tongue, York Ham
Russian Salad
Peaches Melba, Golden Figs
Cheese – Cheshire, Camembert, Kraft
Toast Imperial, Assorted Biscuits
Coffee

This standard of cabin service was maintained to the end of the Empire Air Mail Programme in June 1940 when Italy declared war on the United Kingdom.

LEFT Passengers' dinner menu. *(British Airways Speedbird Heritage Centre)*

ABOVE **Passengers board *Cordelia*.** *(British Airways Speedbird Heritage Centre)*

techniques needed to get items of food, hot or cold, out of the vacuum flasks intact. Poached eggs required a special knack.

A wine list was carried, together with the usual range of spirits. Cocktails were available, including the famous 'Airways Special' (composition unknown). Cigarettes were on sale. Free of charge items included such drinks as tea, cocoa, coffee, chocolate, Bovril, OXO, Horlicks, as well as sandwiches, cocktail snacks, biscuits, fresh fruit, aspirin, smelling salts, eau de Cologne, Enos fruit salts, cotton wool for the ears, barley sugar, saccharine, Glucose-D, air-sickness tablets, soap and towels, pencils, notepaper headed with the aircraft's name, badge and quotation, postcards, and descriptive booklets of the route and night stops. On loan for the flight were playing cards, crossword puzzles, jigsaw puzzles, books, children's magazines, games, and sunglasses.

At stops, the steward was also expected to help make fast any of the servicing craft if required and to tidy up the cabins.

On the water

That flying boats are hybrids is evident from their handling characteristics at low speed on the water, especially when leaving or taking up moorings. For a flying boat, both the tide and the wind play their parts, depending on their relative strengths. Weather conditions also included the state of the water at terminals, as the 'boats could operate in sea states that the attendant servicing vessels could not tolerate.

In the case of sand and dust storms, the visibility at the alighting area decided whether a departure was made.

The Empire 'boats handled well on the water. Taxiing presented no particular difficulties even in cross winds, rough water, adverse tides or currents. The normal engine speed for taxiing was 1,000rpm, with a little more on the upwind engines in crosswind conditions. Lower engine speeds could cause the spark plugs to oil up, sometimes cured by running the faltering engine up to 2,000rpm in rich mixture for a while. Often when taxiing on rough water, the inner engines were throttled back to prevent spray being thrown up on to the airscrew discs.

A fully loaded 'boat had a tendency to swing into the wind on the starboard side when taxiing, and the downwind float could become submerged in rough conditions, making it necessary to ease up into the wind to prevent it being 'lost'. With no brakes, other than the drogues (which could be streamed from the mooring hatch in the nose of the aircraft to assist a turn or to slow – but not stop – a 'boat) the crew had to anticipate continually to avoid difficult situations. Taxiing away from a 'tight' mooring was done with the two outer engines to gain maximum control with the least way, bringing in a third engine if necessary for a turn.

Turning into the wind was normally done with the outer engine, helped by the inner if required, with same-side rudder and opposite aileron. Turning downwind was done with the appropriate engine, or engines, with opposite rudder and same-side aileron.

To turn 180° across a strong wind, it was necessary to swing the 'boat with the engines in the opposite direction to the turn, at the same time applying opposite aileron and rudder, as the engines on the outside of the turn were opened up. The swing had to be checked, as the 'boats had a tendency to turn back into the wind.

Surface vessels at moorings normally lie to the tide or current, whereas flying boats usually lie to the wind. In restricted anchorages, the situation could be difficult. The northward current of the River Nile could be up to 5kts, with a 20kt wind in the opposite direction. In these conditions, the tendency was to lie across the stream, making it impossible to get a tender alongside. A large drogue attached to the 'boat's tail release hook to act as a sea anchor, steadied the aircraft. Once slipped the drogue was recovered by the tender. The use of this simple device completely revolutionised operations on the river.

Lamp signals from the control tender were a flashing green light ('cleared to taxi'); a steady red light ('stop' – difficult or impossible for a flying boat); a flashing red light ('move clear of alighting area'); a flashing white light ('return to starting point').

The signal inside the 'boat for 'let go forward' was given by the captain's whistle, the letter 'L' in Morse code. At the signal, the bowman (usually the radio officer), standing by in the open

mooring hatch, would free the hawser from the bollard with the slip line, raise his hand to indicate to the captain that the hawser had been slipped, retract the bollard, close the mooring hatch, stow the slip line and return to his station on the control deck. On the order 'let go aft', the first officer released the hook under the tail by pulling the lever on the roof of the coupé, confirming the slip, 'all gone aft' to the captain. The 'boat was then free to move. Empire 'boats could be towed, with the tow rope made fast to the retractable mooring bollard.

The draught at the main step for a Mk I S.23 'boat at 40,500lb displacement was 4.1813ft in salt water. The draught at the rear step was approximately half that of the main step. The maximum draught for some of the S.30 'boats with displacements of 53,000lb was 4.62ft in fresh water. The risk of grounding, therefore, was not usually of great concern to 'boats moving normally about their business on the water.

Flying boats were considered to be surface vessels while on the water. As vessels measuring under 150ft in length, they were required to carry an anchor, or riding, light, a steaming light, and an overtaking light – all white, as well as their red and green navigation lights.

The anchor light was required by international law to be visible all round for a distance of two miles. The steaming light was required to have a visibility, from the front of the aircraft, of three miles, in an arc that extended 112° on either side, making a total of 225°. On the Empire 'boats both lights were in a combined fitting at the top of the ensign mast, nested inside the aerial mast. The tail light doubled as an overtaking light while the 'boat was on the water, with an arc of visibility of 67° on either side of the aircraft's centre line, making a total sweep of 135°. The navigation lights had the same arc of visibility as the steaming light. There was a relaxation for British flying boats covering the 'not under command' lights and for fog sound signals such as whistles and bells, although the Boeing 314s carried both.

Starting engines

Starting engines was a two-man operation by the captain and first officer. On the captain's order 'Stand by for starting engines', both pilots checked to see that all was clear of the

BELOW Releasing
Caribou's hawser
from the mooring
bollard. *(British Airways
Speedbird Heritage
Centre)*

airscrews by leaning out of the direct vision panels on their side.

The captain moved the four throttle levers forward about an inch, checked that the mixture controls were 'normal' and that the airscrews were in 'fine' pitch. He then gave the first officer the starting order, which likely would have been: 'Port outer, starboard outer, port inner, starboard inner.'

The first officer left his seat and moved aft to the forward spar frame bulkhead to prime (or dope) the engines. For ground or battery-boat starts, the Dizzy was screwed out and the changeover switch to ground plug. For starts on the aircraft's batteries, the Dizzy was screwed in and the changeover switch to batteries.

Before doping the engines, the first officer checked that the engine cooling gills were wound to the full 'open' position at the two operating positions on either side of the control deck. He checked the two carburettor air intake shutter control wheels were at 'hot air'. A standard Mk I S.23 'boat had a 1D fuel system, with a tank in each mainplane. He opened the fuel tank cocks mounted on the roof, 'green', 'black', and 'red', and confirmed 'All fuel cocks open, connected to common supply.' The common supply was controlled by the 'black'-headed lever, which opened the cock on the balance line and connected together the tanks in each mainplane.

The Ki-gass primers were on either side of the control deck, near the engine cooling gill handles. Each primer consisted of a pump and a cock, which was turned to select one or other of the engines on that side. The priming operation started by operating the plunger of the primer, until the suction pipe and pump were primed full of aviation spirit. The cock was turned to the first engine to be primed and the pump given six full pumping strokes for normal temperature conditions. An extra stroke was given in winter conditions for the outboard engines, but only four strokes were necessary for high summer temperatures. Inboard engines required four pumping strokes for normal conditions, an extra stroke for winter, and only three for high summer. The spring-loaded cock K (for fuel systems 1/1D) or J (for the other systems) was released momentarily to allow the spirit to flood the carburettor of the engine.

Before the engines were started, the flight clerk donned his life jacket, took the Pyrene fire extinguisher in hand from its position on the roof of the control deck near the escape hatch and made his way up the ladder to the escape hatch in the top of the hull. From there he had a clear view of the engines across the top of the mainplanes. If one of the engines should catch fire on starting, he was required to extinguish it. To do this he had to get to the engine, insert the nozzle of the extinguisher into the port in the side of the nacelle, and douse the fire. This was not the easiest of jobs on a slippery mainplane with no handholds, and some of the other engines probably already running – and sometimes in the dark or the rain.

Having primed the first engine, the first officer called out to confirm 'Port outer primed.' The four starter buttons were grouped on the top of the dashboard under a flip-up cover. The cover was engraved with 'Are all hatches closed?' and 'Are all boats clear?' The starter button energised a solenoid switch connecting the starter motor directly to either the 12-volt side of the main battery for an internal start or to the ground plug for an external start. At the same time, the starter button activated the booster coil, direct to the distributor on the engine. The captain pulled the ganged double (port side engines) Lundberg ignition switch upwards for 'on' and held the starter button 'down' until the engine fired, when it was immediately released. If the engine did not fire within 10sec, the button was released and he would wait 30sec before a second try.

Once the engine fired and was running, the throttle lever was advanced to give between 400 and 600rpm. The other three engines were then started in turn. The first officer, back in his seat after priming the engines, watched the engine speeds, the oil temperatures, and the oil pressures. The Record Cirscale engine speed indicators started to register at 500rpm, enabling the first officer to call the engine speeds. Once all the airscrews were turning, the flight clerk retreated down the ladder, closing and securing the hatch behind him and reporting 'Hatch closed' to the captain.

After all the engines had been running for a minute, the captain moved the throttle levers forward to open the engines up to about 700 or 800rpm and then, after a further minute, to 1,000rpm, providing the oil temperatures were above 15°C and the pressures had settled down. The oil pressure gauges were on the starboard panel of the dashboard in front of the first officer, and the temperature gauges on the panel behind his right shoulder. Typical oil pressures when starting from cold were 200 to 150psi, stabilising at about 80psi. The engines would be left at that speed for a further minute before being increased to 1,200rpm, ready for taxiing.

Taking off

The Certificate of Airworthiness allowed the Mk I S.23s to take off loaded to 40,500lb. The loaded weights of the S.30 and S.33 'boats at take-off were increased first to 46,000lb, then 48,000lb, and finally 53,000lb.

If there was a flare path, the 'boat was either guided or towed out to the start by a control tender, or found its own way there. The aircraft was brought up to the threshold of the path about 100yd short of the first flare, and lined up with the path.

When the 'boat was ready to depart, the flight clerk made his final check that all members of the engineering staff had left the aircraft. Starting with the aft passenger hatch, he withdrew the fender and made fast the hatch, made his way forward to the pantry to check that the loading hatch was secured, checked each lavatory (for stowaways) and moved to the forward passenger hatch, withdrawing the fender and securing the hatch. Before reporting 'All passengers seated and hatches fast' to the first officer, he stowed the fenders in the mooring compartment. All hatches on the lower deck were secured.

Directly the engine checks were completed, and oil and cylinder head temperatures were past their minima, oil temperature 15°C minimum, cylinder head temperature 100°C minimum, and oil pressure 70psi minimum for the Pegasus XC engines, the 'boat was ready to take off.

The elevator tab settings depended on the position of the centre of gravity. With the centre of gravity forward at the 55.6in position, the setting for take-off was 'neutral'. With the centre of gravity in the optimum position of 59in the tabs were set at 5½ 'nose down'. In the extreme aft position at 66.9in the setting was 8 'nose down'.

If there was a control tender in attendance, the first officer requested take-off permission. The request, 'OKTO', was made with the signalling lamp in Morse code, in white light. A steady white light from the tender gave permission to take off, confirming that the area had been checked for floating debris. A steady red light from the tender indicated 'stay where you are'.

On the steady white light, the captain would call 'Override in.' The first officer confirmed this and moved the mixture controls back through the throttle gate to the 'full boost' position. The captain took control, moving the control column fully back and opening the throttles slowly and smoothly. If the Exactors were easy, the captain

BELOW Empire 'boat *Champion* of BOAC, takes off from the harbour at Mombasa, Kenya. *Champion* was the first of the improved Empire 'boats that were re-engined with the Bristol Perseus XII C, helping them to carry a greater payload than the S.23. *(Imperial War Museum CH14759)*

moved all the levers together, little by little. If they were stiff, they were opened in pairs, first the outer engines, followed by the inners. The 'boats had a marked tendency to swing to starboard in the early stages of the take-off run, until they were through the 'hump'. The swing was counteracted by retarding the port outer engine, or both engines. Once rudder control became positive at about 40kts, the throttle levers for the retarded engine, or engines, could be pushed forward to the full 'open' position and the 'boat kept straight with the rudder.

Pegasus engines could be run at a maximum speed of 2,475rpm with +3¾psi boost for not more than two minutes. Whenever circumstances allowed, the Empire 'boats made their take-off run directly into the wind. In a crosswind take-off, the outer engines were opened up first and adjusted to get the aircraft to run straight, then the inner engines were fully opened up. Once aileron control became effective at about 40kts, the ailerons were used to keep the 'boat steady as the speed increased. In a 10kt crosswind, full aileron was required, and with a lightly loaded aircraft it was sometimes difficult to hold the windward wing down during the early stages of the take-off. Getting off with a full load at high temperatures was a lengthy process, especially if the water surface was glassy.

The control column was held hard back as the 'boat gathered speed, and then progressively eased forward to the neutral position as the 'boat rose in the water, with the nose kept up to prevent any tendency to lose control. Allowing the nose to dig in produced a 'water loop', with consequent damage if left to build up. The aircraft, still accelerating, was gradually eased up out of the water until it was skimming the surface, with just the point of the main step in contact. It could then be flown

ABOVE *Corsair* **begins her take-off run on the Sea of Galilee.** *(US Library of Congress)*

BELOW An Empire 'boat is watched by the control tender as her speed builds. *(British Airways Speedbird Heritage Centre)*

off the water with a gentle backward pressure on the control column at about 75kts. The minimum take-off speed was 68kts.

Once off the water, the 'boat was held down close to the surface, allowing the air speed to build up to about 95kts before being pulled up to climb away. The take-off and climb out was considered satisfactory at all ports, except for some on the upper reaches of the River Nile, where the proximity of the riverbanks caused some anxious moments.

As the 'boat climbed away from Southampton Water at the start of an Empire

ABOVE *Centurion* **reaches the end of her take-off run on the Sea of Galilee before climbing away.** *(US Library of Congress)*

BELOW G-ADHM *Caledonia* **up 'on the step'.** *(British Airways Speedbird Heritage Centre)*

Air Mail Programme, the radio officer would get off the departure signal to Portsmouth control. At the end of the transmission he would switch the motor generator 'off', change the frequency to 333kcs (the international control frequency), and continue to listen out. Listening to the transmissions of other aircraft, he could get an impression of other aircraft in the air, and their approximate whereabouts.

On Southampton Water six amber-coloured electric battery-operated 'flares' formed the flare path – strung out in line as near as possible in the direction of the wind – about 140yd apart with a width marker at the far end. The licence for the water aerodrome was withdrawn in 1958, after Aquila Airways ceased. A similar arrangement existed at Singapore. Where the flare path was not permanent, it was laid from a control tender by dropping lighted kerosene flares over the side at regular intervals, to make a path 750yd long, with four or six flares.

The corrective drill for an engine out of action on take-off took about 20sec. Three-engine take-offs were possible in certain circumstances. If an engine failed during the take-off run after rudder control speed had

been reached, the 'boat was kept straight with the rudder and the failed engine carburettor cock and the ignition both turned 'off'. A 'boat could take off and be kept straight with the rudder until it gained a safe height. The rudder was then trimmed to take the strain off the rudder bar. If there was a full load on board, there was no chance of climbing away.

Canopus (Captain F.J. Bailey) experienced failure of the port inner engine while over the Mediterranean between Mirabella and Athens on 23 June 1937. The aircraft was put down on the sea and taxied back to Mirabella. The defective engine was removed and the nacelle blanked off with a faired nosing. The port wing float was filled with 5gal of water to balance the 'boat and it took off with the three operational engines. *Canopus* was escorted on its journey back to Rochester by *Cambria*, which had difficulty keeping station with the lightly loaded *Canopus* flying on its three engines.

Centaurus was taken off Lake Tiberias by Captain J.W. Burgess with a dead port outer engine, the main engine bearing having seized. The nearest replacement engine was at Alexandria, and as he wished to get back to the UK as soon as possible, Captain

Burgess decided not to wait for it. There were no passengers on board as the aircraft was returning from the survey flight to New Zealand. The first attempts to take off with three engines failed, as the starboard outer engine could not be fully opened up. The lake was mirror calm and the dead engine's windmilling airscrew generated too much drag, so it was unshipped overnight and stowed in the passenger accommodation. Captain Burgess tried an operational procedure learnt during his days on the Rangoon 'boats. He mustered the crew forward on the lower deck with instructions to

ABOVE *Cambria* **alights on the River Nile at Rod-el-Farag flying boat base, Cairo.** *(IWM CH014781)*

BELOW *Caribou* **takes off from Botwood, Newfoundland, on one of the Atlantic survey flights.** *(British Airways Speedbird Heritage Centre)*

proceed (run) aft as quickly as possible on the word of command. Alone on the upper deck, he opened the throttles. As the 'boat came up on to the step, the crew rushed aft at their captain's shout of command, and *Centaurus* came off the surface 'like a bird'.

In the air

The effective maximum rate for the first segment climb to 1,000ft was 725ft/min. For a fully loaded Mk I S.23 'boat, climbing at 104kts the more usual rate of climb with passengers on board was 400ft/min. From 1,000ft to 10,000ft the maximum rate of climb was 920ft/min, with airscrews in 'coarse' pitch, at an engine speed of 2,000rpm, with +1¼psi boost. By the time a 'boat had reached this height, the rate of climb had dropped to 600ft/min. A height of 10,000ft could be reached in 12½ minutes.

Increasing the all-up weight to 43,000lb decreased the rate of first segment climb to 575ft/min and the maximum rate of climb to 775ft/min. The 'boats had a quirk by which, if the throttles were opened to increase speed during the climb the plane would level off until the increased speed was reached, and then resume its climb.

At a height of 400ft and climbing, the override

BELOW Passengers relax in flight. *(British Airways Speedbird Heritage Centre)*

would be taken 'out' and the mixture control levers moved forward through the gate to the 'normal' position, and the flaps brought 'in'. After checking the oil temperatures and pressures, the engines would be throttled back to 2,200rpm. As the engines changed from the 'full' throttle – 'full' boost condition – to 'normal' boost, the engine note dropped to more usual sound levels. The airscrews were then changed from 'fine' to 'coarse' pitch, and on doing so the aircraft would drop away 50ft in height, before resuming its climb. The first officer adjusted the throttle levers to reduce the engine speed to 2,100rpm and moved the mixture levers to a boost of +1¼psi. The two inner engines were synchronised by ear and the outer engines by eye on either side, adjusting the outer engine speed until the patterns of the airscrew discs coincided. At night the signalling lamp was used to synchronise the engine speeds by shining the beam across the two airscrew discs and adjusting the throttles until the patterns were similar.

At the top of the climb, the aircraft was levelled off and the engines adjusted for economic cruise. The mixture controls were advanced from 'normal' to the 'full weak' position, waiting for the engine speed to drop to 2,130rpm, and then slowly opening the throttles to bring the engine speeds back to 2,200rpm. The directional gyro needed to be checked every 15 minutes to find it, typically, 3° off course. Turning the rudder knob until the bottom card matched the course previously set on the top card brought this back.

At cruising height, the fuel cocks were changed to cruising positions. The first officer left his seat and moved to the fuel cocks mounted at roof level on the spar bulkhead. For the System 1/1D fuel tanks fitted to the Mk I S.23 'boats, he closed the 'black' fuel cock sandwiched between the port and starboard tank cocks, shutting off cock G on the balance line that connected the fuel tanks in each mainplane. The engines on each side then drew their fuel from the tank on that side.

The carburettor air controls – port and starboard – were left at 'cold'. The cylinder head temperatures were adjusted to about 180°C by cranking the port and starboard engine cowl gill handles, to open or close the gills.

The throttles required priming in flight, at the

top of the climb, and thereafter every half-hour into the flight. Priming involved moving the levers forward to 'full open' holding them there for a few seconds and then back to the original position.

The 'boats were unpressurised, so flew all of their working lives in the weather. By all accounts, once in the air the Empire 'boats were a delight to fly. While the individual 'boats differed slightly from each other in their handling and performance, the S.23s, the S.30s and the S.33s all responded in much the same way to the controls and had no recorded vices. Some aircraft were a little slower than the norm, some a little nose heavy, and some more reluctant to leave the water than others.

Forward and centre cabins were considered to be the most uncomfortable for passengers in bumpy conditions. Airsickness among passengers and crew was not uncommon in rough weather, and the 'boats carried cuspidors (spittoons), rather than airsickness bags. In rough weather, the automatic pilot was disengaged and both pilots flew the aircraft together, using combined maximum force. This afforded some relief to the passengers in the aft cabin, as the continual angular motion in pitch, bank, and yaw with the automatic pilot engaged, tended to upset the most hardened travellers. The elevators were not quite fast enough in rough weather, requiring constant elevator trim tab work.

The Certificate of Airworthiness states that:

The seaplane handles well in the air. The elevator control is light and effective over the whole speed range. The aileron control is moderately light and effective at normal speeds but becomes heavier as the speed increases, being quite heavy at top speed. The rudder control is heavy but effective at all speeds. There is ample rudder control with either outer engine throttled.

The elevator and aileron controls for all types of Empire 'boat were well harmonised and, considering the size of the aircraft, gentle. In calm air the Empire 'boats were very stable, especially laterally, and could be easily trimmed hands and feet off. The acceptance trials required the 'boat to fly straight and level 'in normal weather conditions', hands and feet off, for at least ten minutes with a full load on all four engines at cruising speed. When trimmed, the trial was repeated with any one of the engines 'switched off'.

The rudder was not much used in calm air turns and banks, but was used in conjunction with the ailerons in rough weather to prevent distortion of the airframe. The controls reacted more slowly at heights over 10,000ft, and at the service ceiling of 20,000ft they were definitely

BELOW Elevator controls. *(Shorts)*

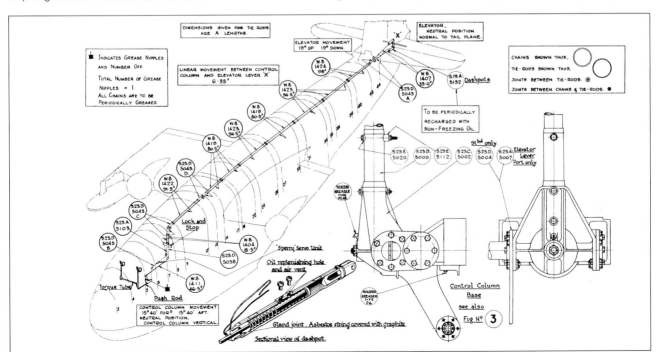

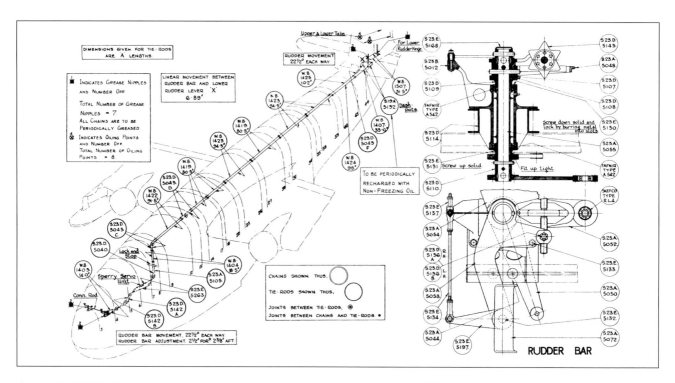

ABOVE Rudder controls. *(Shorts)*

BELOW Aileron controls. *(Shorts)*

sluggish. Although they were approaching the upper limit of size for an aircraft with manual controls, the 'boats could be flown manually for long periods. Captains Loraine and May brought *Clyde* back to the UK from West Africa with an unserviceable automatic pilot, flying manually for more than 3,000 nautical miles – more than 20 hours' flying. The normal arrangement when flying manually was for each pilot to fly a 20- to 30-minute spell, before handing over.

The trim tabs for the elevators and rudder were satisfactory. Climbing out at 104kts, the tab was set to 1 'down', for full-throttle level flight to 7 'down', and in the level cruise to 5 'down'. At the other extreme of the centre of gravity range, the take-off and initial climb was made with 8 'down', full-throttle level flight with 9¾ 'down', and in the cruise with 8¾ 'down'.

In the early days of the EAMP, Captain L.A. Egglesfield decided to find out how high an

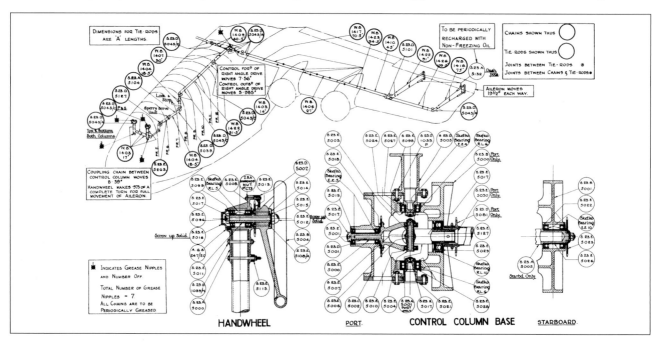

Empire 'boat would go. The 'boat was over the Mediterranean between Marseilles and Lake Bracciano, carrying mail only. Climbing on the automatic pilot the 'boat ascended steadily to the quoted service ceiling of 20,000ft. If crewmembers sat quite still, they experienced no ill-effects from the lack of oxygen, so with the 'boat still climbing it was allowed to have its head, gaining 25,000ft and still climbing slowly. Captain Egglesfield decided that this was high enough for an unpressurised aircraft, and turned the elevator knob to descend.

The quoted service ceilings were revised when the 'boats were in line service. At the standard all-up weight of 40,500lb on four engines the ceiling was 15,500ft; at 41,500lb the ceiling was 14,300ft; at 42,500lb at 13,400ft; and at 43,500lb at 12,300ft. With three engines, the respective figures were 8,000ft, 7,000ft, 6,400ft, and 5,700ft.

The 'boats would dive without vibration or instability up to 200mph (174kts) indicated or about 183kts true, with the throttles ⅔ open, and would pull out easily and quickly. The maximum speed in level flight at 5,500ft was 172kts. The flaps were not fully extended over 100kts.

The normally quoted cruising speed was 143kts at 510bhp per engine, dropping to an economic cruising speed of 128kts at 10,000ft. The optimum cruising speed for maximum range in still air was 114kts. Against the standard 35kt headwind, the optimum speed was 120kts.

The stalling speed with the flaps unextended was 63kts. With ½ flap the stall was at 71kts, with ¾ flap the stall occurred at 70kts, and with full flap the stalling speed was a little over that of the 'clean' condition, at 65kts. The minimum flying speed was 61kts, and the lowest possible alighting speed 59kts.

If an engine went out of action in flight in hot weather at heights over 5,000ft, it became difficult to maintain height, and plenty of control was needed. If the two starboard engines failed, the flutter of the rudder could not be controlled at speeds approaching 130kts and the loss of height was very rapid. A straight course could be kept without rudder flutter if the two port engines were lost, but the loss of height was more than 300ft/min.

Three-engine performance with a heavily laden 'boat was unsatisfactory with a full fuel load, until a sufficient quantity had been burnt off. A 'boat loaded to 48,000lb could not maintain height on three engines. For this reason the long-range 'boats – the original Mk III S.23 'Atlantic' 'boats, the second generation Mk III S.30 long-range 'boats, and the two Mk IV TEAL S.30 'A' 'boats – were fitted with fuel jettison pipes to dump fuel from the inboard mainplane tanks.

The state of the fuel supply was checked every half-hour by 'dipping' the tanks with the Telelevel fuel gauges – another trip for the first officer to the forward spar bulkhead. The first officer was also responsible for the half-hourly instrument report on Form D96. A typical, but considerably simplified, entry might have been:

Time	05.00
Trip clock	1hr 30min
ASI (speed)	155mph
Altimeter (height)	10,000ft
Engine speed ind.	2,200rpm
Boost gauge	−1⅛psi
Oil pressure gauge	80psi
Oil temp gauge	62°C
Cylinder head temperature	160°C
Outside air temperature	+3°C
Sperry oil pressure	13ft lb/sq in
Battery voltage	30 volts

Returning to his seat, he would report the fuel state and the total consumption per hour to the captain.

As the 'boats had limited ability to fly round or over the weather, they were frequently in the thick of it. During the first winter of operation with IAL, the Empire 'boats had no external protection from icing. Warm front conditions were especially dangerous. Thunderclouds could form behind the line of flight, making it impossible to

turn back. Climbing to get over the clouds also had its problems, as fast-moving cumulus could out-climb a 'boat, especially as the 'boat's rate of climb dropped off with altitude. It was not uncommon for the 'boats, unpressurised and with marginally effective heating systems and no oxygen available, to be taken to 18,500ft over France in the early days of the service to avoid turbulence and ice. Captains Burgess and Caspareuthus were reputed to hold the joint height record of 22,000ft with passengers on board. IAL's passengers – comatose, well wrapped up, uncomplaining, and ignorant of anoxia – accepted high-altitude flying as one of the hazards of the journey. The leading women's magazine suggested that the lady passengers would be grateful for a warm coat in case it should be necessary for their aircraft to climb to 18,000ft crossing France. Experience with the route brought increasing confidence and more comfortable flight levels, so it became less common to climb to those heights.

Although the choke tube of the carburettor was heated by circulating hot engine oil round the jacket, and heat could also be applied to the carburettor air intake, the heating arrangements were often not effective. In certain cloud conditions, the engines faded as the edge of the cloud touched them and the 'boat had to climb to avoid the carburettors becoming iced up. A 'boat could be chased up to over 20,000ft in this fashion over the Massif Central, on the Southampton to Marignane sector. *Cavalier* was lost on 21 January 1939 over the North Atlantic, about halfway between Bermuda and Baltimore, because of loss of power from carburettor icing. Storms over sectors of the African, Middle East, and Indian routes could be sudden and violent. In rough weather the 'boats were quite stable, tending to pitch in a not unpleasant way. In patches of rough weather, 'bumps' of 3g occurred, those of 2g were common, and occasionally 'bumps' of 6g were recorded in monsoon conditions.

The Empire 'boats were among the first British commercial aircraft to fly with automatic pilots. The 'boats were fitted with Sperry equipment of US origin, except for the two or three 'A' 'boats, which were fitted with British RAE Smiths automatic pilots. It is not known if *Australia/Clare* was fitted with Sperry or Smiths equipment.

ABOVE G-AFRA, *Cleopatra*, circling Durban, South Africa, prior to alighting on the harbour after flying the Horseshoe Route from Sydney, Australia. *Cleopatra* was the last Empire 'boat to be built and was handed over to BOAC in May 1940. *(IWM CH14761)*

The engaging lever was on the rear of the throttle box, with the 'off' position to port and the 'on' position to starboard. The speed valves controlled the flow of oil from the servo units and could be adjusted to suit the speed with which the rudder, the ailerons, and the elevators reacted to the prevailing weather conditions. Spring-loaded relief valves allowed the automatic control to be overpowered by the pilots in emergencies, by the application of about twice the normal manual force.

Before engaging the automatic pilot in the air, the aircraft was trimmed straight and level, the vacuum was checked (4in of mercury), the oil pressure (150psi), speed valves 'open'. The bank-and-climb gyro was uncaged by turning the caging knob anticlockwise to its full extent, and the directional gyro by pushing the caging knob 'in', turning it to set the lower card to the course, and then pulling the caging knob 'out'. The rudder knob on directional gyro control was turned to align the upper and lower cards, and the aileron and elevator knobs turned until the respective follow-up indices matched their indicators. The level control was checked as 'off', then the engaging lever slowly turned over to 'on', the pilot becoming aware of the automatic pilot taking control of the aircraft. The rudder knob was adjusted to bring the aircraft exactly to the course already set. Climb was set by the elevator knob. Turns could be made flat with the rudder knob, or banked with the aileron knob. The automatic pilot could also be disengaged, the turn made manually, and then re-engaged.

Alighting

The descent from cruising altitude was normally between 300 and 400ft/min. If conditions were likely to be bumpy, the descent was quickened to 400ft/min to save the passengers from discomfort. At that rate, the descent from a cruising height of 10,000ft to circuit height took just over 20 minutes, which for most passengers was not sufficient time for them to become airsick.

A left-hand circuit was normally flown over the alighting area at a height of between 800 to 1,000ft at a speed of 120kts giving time for the captain to view the alighting area, for the first officer to prime the throttles and mixture controls in pairs, and for the radio officer to wind in the trailing aerial. The flight clerk went up to the control deck to start moving the mail from the mail room into the square of the hatch, ready for off-loading. Returning to his station on the lower deck, he made the rounds of the passenger cabins with the steward. The passengers put their seats in the fully upright position and secured their seat belts. The flight clerk collected the passengers' passports, tickets, quarantine cards, currency cards, and aliens' cards, and returned to his office in the forward mail room. The passports were placed in the passport container.

On the water below, the control tender turned to point its bow into the wind. A steady green or white light from the surface was the lamp signal for 'clear to alight'. A flashing red lamp signal indicated 'do not alight'. A steady red light was the signal to 'give way' to another aircraft.

A gentle turn to port started the approach, to alight as near as possible into the wind. The usual approach speed was around the 100kt mark in good visibility, or 90kts in marginal conditions. Once the 'boat had been turned and lined up, the airscrews were changed from 'coarse' to 'fine' pitch and the engines throttled back. Flaps could be put out early in the approach as no change of trim was required while they were moving or when extended. The captain called the flap setting and the first officer reached up to the coupé roof to pull the flap motor switch 'on' and moved the controller flaps operating switch down to 'flaps out'.

The 'boat, descending at between 300 to 400ft/min, was kept level with the ailerons. The captain normally had control, and eased back slightly on the control column to momentarily check the descent, and increased the engine speed to 2,300rpm to keep the 'boat's speed up. At 20ft above the surface, he checked the 'boat by moving the control column back and then to the neutral position, at the same time moving the throttle levers practically to the 'closed' position.

In a normal alighting, the aircraft rounded out above the water in a planing attitude and touched down with the point of the main step, followed almost immediately by the point of the aft step. The tail continued to dig into the water and, with the control column hard back, some power was applied to ease it as the way came off and the aircraft came off the step. As the speed dropped off the 'boat settled down into the water, the bow wave increasing until it was washing up the sides of the hull. If the nose rose too high, the inner engines were opened

up momentarily to check it. As the 'boat came off the plane, there was a sensation of 'falling through' the water surface. With the flaps at the ¾ setting, the bow wave often streamed back to beat on the flaps before they could be brought 'in', to be countered by opening up the inner engines for an instant to check it.

The captain called for 'flaps in', the first officer reached up to pull the flap motor switch, 'on (blue light on)' and moved the controller flaps operating switch down to 'flaps in'. As the flaps started to move, he watched the flap position indicator move round the dial, (red light off) as the flaps moved past the 'out' position. With the flaps 'in', he switched off.

Alighting into a 5kt wind with 'full' flap, a typical arrival took about 18 to 20sec with a run of some 350yd. Directly the aircraft was on the water, the flaps were brought 'in'. It took the flap motor 90sec to wind them in from the 'full' flap position.

As the way came off, the captain brought the inboard throttle levers towards the 'closed' position. The 'boat could then taxi to a mooring or take a tow from the control tender. Taxiing in to a mooring or pontoon was done with the two outer engines idling at 200rpm.

The approach to the mooring was made as slowly as possible to give the radio officer, as bowman, the best chance to pick it up first time. The 'boat's way dropped off slowly, so speed was reduced well away from the mooring. Drogues could cut down the speed still further and to help in turning on to a mooring.

If the wind and tide were in the same direction, the approach was made in the usual way without difficulty, up-tide and upwind. In this situation, the mooring buoy would be streaming towards the aircraft and could be easily picked up.

If the approach was made downwind up-tide, the control of the aircraft was as good, but the drogues would be less effective.

When the wind and tide were in opposition, and the approach had to be made across them, the situation was problematic. It was virtually impossible to hold the head of the flying boat to the buoy, so the pick-up had to be quick as the bow was allowed to drift across the buoy. Getting away was as difficult as mooring, and often the mooring cable had to be cut. The 'boats could operate safely in water conditions that were too rough for the attendant surface craft.

When he had finished with the engines, the captain switched the ignition 'off' for all engines and pulled the inboard and outboard engine cut-out levers. The first officer turned each airscrew until one blade was vertical by working the starter button. The rudder bar was centralised, the control wheel levelled, and the control column pushed fully forward, depressing the elevators to their fullest extent so the control lock could be inserted. Moving aft to the forward spar bulkhead, the first officer closed all the fuel cocks and screwed the Dizzy 'out'. While at the bulkhead, he checked the remaining fuel in the tanks. Returning to his seat, he primed the throttle levers by pushing them fully forward and leaving them in 'full open' position, and then the mixture controls by moving the levers back and leaving them there. The carburettor test cocks between the pilot's seats were turned 'off' and the flap closed.

Night alightings were made by setting up the aircraft on the approach in the planing attitude, controlling the rate of descent to 200ft/min with the engines. Only when the aircraft was firmly on the surface was power reduced. The flare path or searchlight of the control tender gave direction and an indication of the surface level.

Alightings sometimes had to be made in sandstorms. Two methods of approaching an alighting area were used, depending on visibility. One was to fly on course by dead reckoning and then lose height to 600ft as the alighting area approached. When the ground was in sight, to follow ground features to the alighting area. The second, with the visibility of more than 800yd, was to fly directly over the alighting area on a radio bearing and then descend to make visual contact with the ground. Aircraft in dust and sandstorms become highly charged, so radio communication was notoriously difficult. Taking off was not recommended if the visibility at the alighting area was less than 300yd.

Late on in the operational lives of the 'boats, Standing Orders were issued for forced alightings over the ocean. When a forced alighting was imminent and inevitable, the aircraft's course was altered to the nearest sheltered water, ship, or shipping lane. A distress signal was to be sent and

radio transmission continued for as long as possible. After the last position report, the radio transmitting key was to be clamped down to transmit continuously. Freight was to be jettisoned if the loss of weight would mitigate the circumstances. Life rafts or dinghies were not part of the equipment of the original IAL 'boats, but were included later. If an emergency alighting was to be made, rafts were prepared along with emergency rations, water, a signal pistol and cartridges, navigating equipment, and a chart with the last known position marked.

ABOVE Passengers disembark from *Challenger* on to the tender that will convey them to the terminal. *(British Airways Speedbird Heritage Centre)*

LEFT The Imperial Airways flying boat terminal at Darrel Island, Bermuda. *(British Airways Speedbird Heritage Centre)*

BELOW Refuelled and restocked, *Challenger* waits at her moorings as its passengers embark for the start of their journey. *(British Airways Speedbird Heritage Centre)*

Chapter Seven

Maintaining the 'C' class

Basic maintenance checks could be carried out on an Empire 'boat while moored in harbour, but more extensive work would necessitate the attachment of beaching gear to enable it to be hauled out of the water and towed into a hangar.

OPPOSITE Empire 'boat *Cordelia* undergoes maintenance with the aid of moveable platforms on both sides. The port inner engine is being run up. *(British Airways Speedbird Heritage Centre)*

Refuelling

The two main methods used for refuelling the 'boats on the water were 'through the side' and 'over the top', and it depended on the type of anchorage and the facilities available at the port as to which one was chosen. In sheltered harbours where a powered refuelling barge was available, the refuelling was normally carried out through the side, via the refuelling cock on the starboard side of the aircraft. In less sheltered harbours and the fast-flowing rivers of Africa, the refuelling was usually done 'over the top', delivering the spirit directly to each tank through its individual filler cap, either by hoseline from a barge, or from cans and drums.

The Empire 'boats were the first British commercial aircraft to use 87-octane aviation spirit to the DTD 230 specification. The crude oil came mostly from Mexico, and the spirit was derived from petroleum with added aromatics and/or tetraethyl lead. The specific gravity was about 0.76, depending on the exact origin of the base stock but often shown on the aircraft weight schedules as 0.74. The boiling point of the spirit was between 50 and 180°C – which caused some problems with vapour locks in the fuel systems in hot weather. The calorific value was between 18,750 and 18,600Btu/lb.

The lubricating oil used for the engines was DTD 109 mineral oil, usually AeroShell 100. The oil was dispensed over the top through the filler

ABOVE *Canopus* is refuelled over the top with the hose over the leading edge of the mainplane, next to the starboard inner engine. *(British Airways Speedbird Heritage Centre)*

BELOW Refuelling operations on the Nile. The starboard outer engine oil tank is being refilled by a measure from cans. *(Author's collection)*

BELOW The first officer checks the oil tank of the starboard inner engine. *(British Airways Speedbird Heritage Centre)*

caps of individual oil tanks by pipeline from the refuelling barge or by measures from cans.

The Shell Company ordered 27 self-propelled steel refuelling barges for the Empire routes. The barges were 50ft long by 10ft wide by 3ft 6in draught with a freeboard of 4ft 9in and a speed of 7kts. A full load of aviation spirit was 2,500gal in four tanks, two 500gal tanks and two 750gal tanks. Lubricating oil was carried in two 200gal tanks.

A single barge carried enough spirit and oil to service a 'boat with any fuel system except System M1. The aviation spirit pump on the barge was a Stothert & Pitt rotary displacement pump, delivering 120gal/min at a pressure of 25psi through a Kent indicating meter. The lubricating oil was delivered by compressed air through a flexible hoseline at between 7 and 10gal/min, depending on the viscosity of the oil.

The normal crew complement of a refuelling barge was a coxswain (in charge of the barge and responsible for seamanship), a pump man (responsible for the refuelling operation), and a deckhand (whose duties included mooring the barge, casting off, and generally assisting with the refuelling).

Refuelling was a potentially hazardous operation. Heavily laden refuelling barges, even when powered, were not the sprightliest of vessels. Away from the main bases, the seamanship of the barge coxswains was not always up to the standards of Southampton Water, and although the barges were well provided with fenders, when a collision occurred between a barge and an aircraft, it was inevitably the aircraft that was damaged.

Mishandling of a mooring or casting-off operation could also cause the retractable main bollard at the aircraft's mooring hatch to be wrenched out of position.

The more important ports along the routes had resident British station officers who supervised the refuelling operation. At other ports, it was the first officer who took the responsibility for supervision.

At the start of the first service of the day, the aircraft would have been fuelled before the passengers boarded. It was IAL policy that no passengers were allowed to remain on board while aircraft were being refuelled. At intermediate stops, passengers were either taken ashore or, weather and circumstances permitting, treated to a sightseeing trip in an IAL tender until the refuelling had been completed.

The amount of fuel required for the sector about to be flown was established, the contents

of the tanks checked by the aircraft's gauges (or by dipping the tanks), and the total fuel uplift calculated. Aircraft that had recently flown through sand or dust storms were highly charged with static electricity, so extra care was required during the refuelling.

If the refuelling were to be through the side, the supervisor would open up the mail loading hatch on the starboard side of the control deck. From this position he had a good view of the refuelling barge as it tied up immediately below him. The aircraft's main electrical switchboard, the fuel gauges, and tank cocks were all within his easy reach. The supervising officer (the station officer or first officer) checked that the Dizzy was screwed right 'out', that all switches on the main switchboard were 'off', that the tank cocks were 'closed' and that the fire extinguishers on the control deck were ready for action. The ladder leading to the escape hatch in the top of the hull was also close by. The

disruption caused by the refuelling operation was one of the reasons for the flight clerk moving from the control deck to an office in the forward cabin on the deck below.

The refuelling cock was installed in its fuel-proof box, complete with door, let into the outside of the starboard hull plating of the aircraft above the pantry loading hatch. The cock had a four-position body with an operating handle, which could be turned to select 'starboard', 'both sides', 'port', or 'all off' – allowing fuel to be pumped to the tank, or tanks, on either side of the aircraft, or to both sides simultaneously. The 'all off' position was selected when refuelling had been completed to allow the system to drain down. Refuelling through the cock was carried out under pressure of the pump on the refuelling barge. To withstand this pressure, the refuelling pipelines were run from the refuelling cock to the various tanks in duralumin tubing. In the flight-refuelled 'boats the pipeline from the tail cup, where fuel entered the aircraft from the tanker, ran to the two inboard tanks in the same tubing.

The fuel systems could be drained down through the refuelling cock by the drain line. Almost any fuel tank, or the whole system if necessary, could be drained down through the refuelling cock via the drain line, with the exception of the small 204gal hull tank in System M1.

The refuelling operation started with the refuelling barge approaching the aircraft's starboard bow and standing off. The signal that all was ready on the aircraft was a long blast on the whistle. A powered refuelling barge would come alongside the 'boat and tie up on its starboard side. A mooring line from the bowman on the barge would be taken to the aircraft's bow mooring hatch and made fast to the retractable bollard. If the tide were running at more than 2kts, an additional line would be secured to the storm pennant. The barge's line aft would be made fast to the mooring cleats let into the side of the aircraft. The barge was then immediately below the mail loading hatch, in a position to make the connection to the refuelling cock in the starboard side of the aircraft.

When the wind and the tide were from the same direction it was not difficult for the barge

BELOW *Calypso* **taking on fuel on Lake Habbaniyah in Iraq. The Shell fuel tender is moored under the starboard mainplane so that the connection can be made to the 'boat's refuelling cock.** *(British Airways Speedbird Heritage Centre)*

to approach and close with the moored aircraft, approaching from aft, upwind and up-tide, to tie up alongside the starboard side of the flying boat. When the wind and tide were in opposite directions the situation was more difficult. The barge could either approach the flying boat from aft down-tide, anchor and warp back to it, or approach up-tide from the aircraft's head, a decision that depended on the strength of the tide and the skill of the coxswain. When the wind and tide were across each other the situation was even more problematic, and sometimes impossible.

Before connecting to the refuelling cock, the spirit in the barge's tanks was checked for water. The first gallon of spirit from each of the barge's tanks was pumped through a chamois leather into a bucket, any water from the tanks being revealed and retained by the leather.

The pump man on the barge watched the Kent meter to monitor the flow. The rate of pumping was reduced towards the end of the operation so that the last 20gal was pumped slowly into the tanks. The Relunit valves inside the tanks were designed to close off when the tanks were full. In fact, they could often be heard to close, with an audible 'clunk', before the tank was absolutely full. When this happened, the pump man would be watching the connecting hose, ready to disengage the clutch on the delivery pump motor at the first sign of bulging, before the pump pressure could do any damage. By turning the refuelling cock first to 'starboard' and then to 'port' and pumping very slowly, the last 10gal of spirit could be 'squeezed' past the Relunit valves to fill the tanks. The tank vents acted as overflows, discharging surplus fuel through the under-surface of the mainplanes.

When the fuel tanks were full, the 'boat's system was drained by turning the refuelling cock to the 'both sides' position and opening the drain cock on the aircraft, allowing the residual spirit in the refuelling lines (about 2gal in the 1/1D fuel system) to run back through the cock to clear the lines. The hose from the barge was disconnected, the refuelling cock turned to 'all off' and the door to the recess in the side of the aircraft closed and secured. The barge cast off, and the operation was complete.

When refuelling over the top, the fuel was delivered to the filler of each tank, either through a hose from the refuelling barge or directly through funnels from drums. If hoses were used, the barge was either tied up alongside the 'boat on either side or streamed out fore or aft. On swiftly flowing rivers such as the Nile and the Congo, the barges were made fast to the 'boat's mooring bollard or the tail release hook. When the barge was attached forward, the hoses were brought up over the leading edge of the mainplanes. With the barge moored aft, the hoses were brought aboard over the tailplane and along the top of the hull, with the fabric-covered elevators depressed out of harm's way.

Refuelling from drums was a last resort, as they had to be manhandled up on to the mainplanes. Allowing for the state of the wind and tide, the refuelling barge would be moored in the best position to get the drums on board the aircraft without damage. If the drums were on the barge the 'boat could be refuelled from the drums by semi-rotary pump and hoseline.

While the fuel tanks were being filled, the oil tank, or tanks, in each engine nacelle were topped up from the lubricating oil tank on the barge. The flaps in the engine nacelles over the filler and circulating chamber caps were unfastened, the caps unscrewed, and the levels in the oil tanks checked with the dipstick in the circulating chamber. If additional oil was required, this was added through the tank filler. When completed, the caps were screwed back on. The tightness of the caps was crucial, as they had a tendency to seize solid if screwed up too tight. When all the caps were on, the flaps in the nacelles were fastened with a half turn of the fastener.

Refuelling could be carried out in any weather, except that rain during refuelling over the top was an additional hazard. Preparations inside the aircraft were the same as those for refuelling through the side, but with the tank filler covers removed and the filler caps unscrewed. When filling over the top by hose or drums, funnels with chamois leather linings were used to filter out any water present in the spirit. The funnels were earthed with static lines to the aircraft. Over the top, using dipsticks, was the more accurate method.

In-flight refuelling

Flight Refuelling Limited's technique for establishing contact between the receiver and the tanker aircraft is described in detail in Patent 508 220, applied for on 5 January 1938. The two aircraft involved in the refuelling operation were the Handley Page Harrows, acting as the tanker aircraft, and the S.30 Empire 'boats, acting as receivers.

The S.30 'boats, as receiver aircraft, were modified during construction. The extreme end of the tail cone, aft of Frame 51, was altered to take the refuelling cup (Patent 491 953, 10 December 1936) with spring-loaded locking claws around the periphery. The claws were locked by a hydraulically operated manual pump, connected through a pressure release unit designed to break the locking arrangement if the force on the hose exceeded a pull of 1,000lb. Transfers in bumpy or gusty weather could cause the hose nozzle to momentarily break clear of the receiver cup. Methyl bromide fire extinguishers were provided. The drum of the S.30 'boat's winch had 300ft of 10cwt steel wire hauling line wound on to it, the first 75ft of line being of lighter gauge than the hauling line to act as a weak link. For easy operation, the manually operated winch was geared with a ratio of 1:5, and fitted with a brake lever. For the receiver, the whole assembly was mounted inside the hull of the Empire 'boat on the refuelling platform, just forward of Frame 41. The lead weight (16lb) and grapnel attached to the end of the hauling line were housed in the refuelling cup until streamed to make contact with the tanker. As the weight could become jammed in the refuelling cup, the S.30 'boats were fitted with a small hatch cut into the underside of the hull, immediately below the cup, to allow the winch operator to lean out to dislodge it with a special crook. Lookout windows were fitted in place of hull plating in the top of the hull, between Frames 40 and 41 on the starboard side and between Frames 42 and 43 to port. The winch operator and the pilot communicated via light signals. A switchbox with

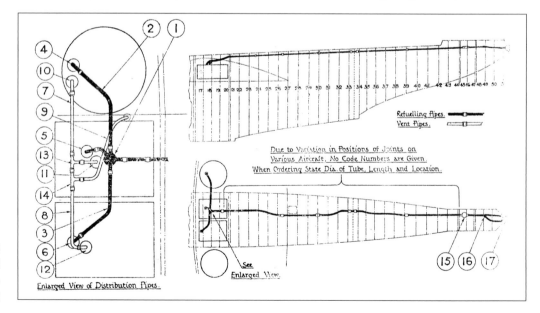

Diagram labels: SEE ENLARGED VIEW OF PANEL. — LOOK OUT WINDOWS. — PIPE LINE TO TANKS — MAIN COCK — LEVER CONTROLLING MAIN COCK — GUARD ROPE — GUIDE TUBE — REFUELLING PLATFORM — WINDLASS. — HAULING LINE. — APPROX. POSITION FOR EMERGENCY RELEASING OF LEAD WEIGHT. — SPECIAL CRANK. — TRAP DOOR REMOTELY CONTROLLED — GUIDE TUBE — HYDRAULIC COUPLING — PIPE LINE TO TANKER — RECEIVER CUP. — TAIL REFUELLING SIGNALS — PRESSURE GAUGE "d" — PRESSURE RELEASE UNIT "b" — HYDRAULIC PUMP "a" — PRESSURE CONTROL VALVE "c" — ENLARGED VIEW OF PANEL.

three switches: No 1 white (meaning 'Tanker in sight'), No 2 green (meaning 'Ready to receive'), and No 3 red (meaning 'Emergency'). The pilot had a similar switchbox on the control deck, switching 'off' to acknowledge. The total weight of the refuelling equipment was about 100lb.

The tanker aircraft was the modified Handley Page Harrow G-AFRL, with a crew of one pilot and two winch operators. The transfer hose reel, with its 175ft of 2in-diameter hose, was fitted in the floor of the fuselage, slightly ahead of the centre of gravity. The hose was led forward over a guide roller to its stowed position, immediately under the pilot's seat. The contact winch was just forward of the guide roller. The fuel carried for transfer was 960gal. Two 125gal transfer tanks were fitted in the fuselage, and the balance of the transfer fuel was held in five 142gal wing tanks, arranged along the plane of the Harrow's centre of gravity. An additional 150gal fuselage tank provided fuel for the tanker's engines. A tank holding 500 litres of nitrogen gas was available for purging the system, to flush the length of the transfer hose through to the claw holes in the refuelling cup in the receiver. The transparent lookout sheeting incorporated apertures for the line-throwing gun aft of the wing and for the signalling flags near the winches.

The tankers did not carry full radio equipment, although they were fitted with direction-finding loops, so that they could home on to the Empire 'boat to establish contact in marginal weather conditions. Communication between the tanker and the receiver during the refuelling operation was by flags, carried by both aircraft. A red flag indicated 'Emergency'; orange 'Transfer of fuel completed'; green 'Ready for transfer'; and chequered black and white 'Break-away'. Flags were flown by rolling them up on the staff, pushing them out into the airstream and releasing them with a twist.

Contact between tanker and receiver was established by firing across the receiver's extended hauling line with a hand-held line-throwing gun. The gun, a Greener cavalry gun, designed in 1880, was adapted to fire a grapnel attached to the end of the Harrow's hauling line, coiled on a Schermuly rocket cable drum. Sir Alan Cobham, in his book *A Time to Fly,* records: 'The recoil of this ancient gun practically threw its operator overboard when we tried it in a Virginia, but a little practice soon made this a very reliable technique.'

The Empire 'boat, as the receiver, flew on course to the rendezvous at the agreed height, straight and level. As the Harrow approached, the receiver's winch operator alerted the pilot (Switch No 1 white 'Tanker in sight') and started to stream the hauling line. The tanker took station slightly behind and below the Empire 'boat, on its starboard quarter. When the receiver's hauling line had been fully streamed, the Harrow would climb so that it was just above the weight on the end of the line. The Greener line-throwing gun was then discharged, so that the contact line from the tanker shot ahead and across the bight in the Empire 'boat's hauling line, and as it was blown back, the lines came in contact with each other. The grapnels at the end of the lines engaged, establishing contact. The connected lines were then hauled in to the Harrow, the Empire 'boat's hauling line transferred to the transfer hose nozzle and the hose allowed to unwind as before. The hose was then wound in to the receiver by the first officer, acting as winchman, in the Empire 'boat. The nozzle was hydraulically locked home in the refuelling cup, the main cock turned 'on', Switch No 2 green 'Ready to receive' turned on, and the green flag flown, acknowledged by a green flag from the Harrow. Purging of the system with nitrogen gas began. The fuel systems in the Harrow, the refuelling hose, and the receiving system in the Empire 'boat were completely flushed through with nitrogen gas to lessen the risk of fire caused by a spark generated by the spirit, as it flowed through the hose. The nitrogen purge was followed by the fuel, flowing by gravity at about 110gal/min. If the hose was pulled away from the tail fitting during the transfer, the break was immediately signalled by the chequered black and white flag, usually by the Empire 'boat first and acknowledged by the Harrow. Once the hose was reconnected by hauling the nozzle back in position and locking it home, a green flag from the 'boat would be acknowledged by the Harrow's own green flag.

When the transfer had been completed, the main cocks in both aircraft were turned 'off', signalled by the orange flag. The nozzle was released from the Empire 'boat by operating the handle on the hydraulic pressure release unit. The receiver cup was flushed with methyl bromide gas, and the hauling line was allowed to unwind to its full extent as the winch operator in the Harrow wound in the hose. The final break was made by the Harrow turning away to break the connection at the weak link on the Empire 'boat's hauling line, well away from any petrol vapour and, should there be any sparking from static, it would be harmless. In all the refuelling operations carried out by FRL and IAL,

no sparks were ever seen. The average time for the contact and transfer was about a quarter of an hour, three to seven minutes for making contact, five minutes to haul down the hose and seven to eight minutes for the transfer of the fuel, averaging about 800gal.

The S.30 'boats *Cabot, Caribou, Connemara,* and *Clyde* were fitted with M1 fuel systems with durations of some 19hr 16min, but only *Cabot* and *Caribou* were fully equipped for flight refuelling. As in all pioneering ventures, problems arose. The three fuel tanks on the Empire 'boats involved in the flight refuelling operation, the two 280gal hull tanks and the starboard 380gal inboard tank did not fill at equal rates, and the fuel from the starboard wing tank siphoned back into the hull tanks. To cure this unforeseen eventuality, sliding valves were fitted to the tank inlets. The starboard wing tank was fitted with a jettison pipe that projected below the hull near the main step. Taking off vibrated the pipe and broke the support, causing the pipe to trail, and on one occasion to fracture one of the plates in the planing bottom. The jettison valve was initially troublesome, as jettisoned fuel was eddying at the main step and washing up the rear of the aircraft as far as the elevators and rudder. The hydraulic system to lock the nozzle in the refuelling cup gave trouble, and breakaways were not uncommon. The first Atlantic air mail service, North Atlantic Westbound 1, was flown by *Caribou* (Captain J.C. Kelly-Rogers) on 5 August 1939 with 454kg of mail. *Caribou* was refuelled at Foynes by the Harrow tanker at 1,000ft in full view of the assembled press. To allow photographs, the two aircraft were flown on a left-hand circular track and, as the Harrow was on the outside, it had difficulty keeping up with the Empire 'boat. Contact was made on the second attempt and there was a breakaway when some fuel was lost during the transfer. The transfer was completed in 16 minutes. Of the 15 transfers during the 1939 North Atlantic trials, NAE 1 was not flight refuelled. Nine transfers were 'good' or 'satisfactory', although fuel got into the hull of the receiver in varying amounts on five occasions. IAL thought that the tankers tended to get too high, perhaps to increase the pressure head and shorten the time for the transfer of fuel, but FRL considered that any problems that arose were because of the 'boats not being properly handled. At least one contact and transfer was made with the Empire 'boat on automatic pilot.

The flight refuelling equipment for the S.30 Atlantic 'boats was installed aft of the freight room at about Frame 42. The equipment included:

- Refuelling platform
- Windlass complete with hauling line and brake
- Receiver cup and guide tube
- Main cock and cock-controlling lever
- Tail refuelling signal box
- Hydraulic pump, pressure control valve, pressure release unit, and pressure gauge
- Special crook for releasing pipeline weight
- Set of signalling flags (red, green, orange, and black and white chequered)

LEFT Port side beaching leg in position. *(Shorts)*

Beaching

When a 'boat was to be beached it was moored by the head until weather conditions were right. On Southampton Water the best time was at high water, although the area off the Hythe slipway was deep enough for an aircraft to be beached at any time, except dead low water and one hour either side of the spring tide highs. The slipway mooring was out of the run of the tide, making handling easier, but a watchful eye had to be kept on the movements of the larger ocean liners, as their wash could cause difficulties at crucial moments during a beaching. Winter conditions, strong

winds at any time of the year, and night-time beachings were added complications.

A beaching crew consisted of a charge hand and six seamen. The beaching chassis was attached while the 'boat was in the water on the slipway mooring. The port and starboard beaching legs were run down the slipway into the water, running on the main and transport wheels, main wheels first. The transport wheel was removed and a line hitched to the strut for towing out to the aircraft.

Once in the water, the struts floated in a wheels-down attitude with the strut at an angle of 60° so that when brought up to the hull of a 'boat, the wheels were under the hull. The strut

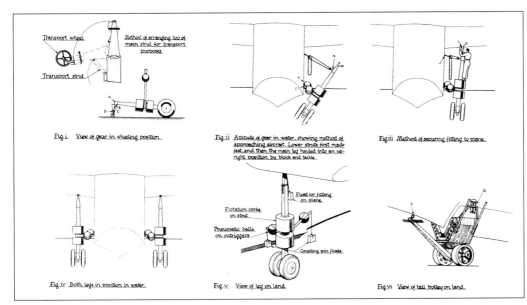

LEFT Beaching equipment. *(Shorts)*

ABOVE *Corsair,* with
her beaching gear
fitted, is hauled up the
slipway at Hythe on
Southampton Water.
Note the line secured
to the 'boat's tail
mooring ring. *(British
Airways Speedbird
Heritage Centre)*

was taken alongside and the attachment pins
on the outriggers inserted in the holes in the hull
at the spar frames (Frames 15/16 and 20/21).
These holes were sealed with watertight plungers
that could be withdrawn from inside the 'boat.
The withdrawal of the plungers and the insertion
of the pins were arranged to coincide, to prevent
any water being shipped. The forward outrigger
strut was attached to its pin first, followed by the
rear outrigger strut. The ring bolt was screwed
home in its socket in the hull and a 10cwt
differential chain block and tackle hooked on to
the ring. The other end of the tackle hooked on
to the beaching strut and the load was taken up
on the chain. One of the beaching crew stood
on the top flotation cork of the strut to work the
block and tackle to bring the strut upright. As
the strut was brought up to the underside of the
mainplane, he inserted the fitting on the underside
of the forward truss of the mainplane spar, where
it was held by two hinged stub pins and locked
by a quarter turn. The chain block was then
removed and passed over for the beaching strut
on the other side to be connected in the same
way. The average time taken to beach a 'boat
was from 15 to 20 minutes, depending on the

weather (particularly the wind), the state of the
tide, and passing ships.

The hauling-out line was attached to the
quick-release hook under the 'boat's tail. The
'boat was brought round until it was floating
in calm water over the slipway, stern towards
the land. The tail trolley was floated out and
forced under the rear step. The adjustable
stub fittings on the trolley were inserted into
the receiving eyes in the hull and screwed up
by the hand-screws. The trolley handle was
lashed to the ring bolt on the centre line of the
hull, and the aircraft was ready to be hauled
out by tractor or winch.

Directly it was clear of the water, the hull was
hosed down to remove any salt deposits. The
security of the beaching chassis was checked
and the 'boat hauled right up the slipway. The
maximum allowable weight of a 'boat on the
beaching chassis was 39,000lb. At the top of
the slip, a tractor took over to tow the aircraft
either directly into one of the hangars, or to
park it on the hard standing outside. With the
tail trolley handle freed, a 'boat on the beaching
chassis could be turned in its own length.
Launching was the reverse of beaching.

Maintenance checks

IAL's main engineering base was the former Vickers Supermarine Works at Hythe, south of Southampton, on the south-west shore of Southampton Water. The Air Ministry bought the works in 1938 as a 'temporary' home, first serving IAL, and later the British Overseas Airways Corporation (BOAC) until it closed on 31 March 1948. Other maintenance bases were established at Alexandria, Kisumu, Durban, Karachi, Calcutta, and Singapore. QEA built a maintenance base at Rose Bay on Sydney Harbour, and TEAL's base was at Mission Bay, Auckland. Durban later became the main base for the Horseshoe Route and grew to become an extensive facility covering the whole range of workshop activities.

ABOVE *Caledonia* **under maintenance at Poole during the war.** (*British Airways Speedbird Heritage Centre*)

LEFT *Coriolanus* **pictured at Rose Bay, Sydney, when she was transferred to QANTAS Empire Airways with the Australian registration VH-ABG.** (*British Airways Speedbird Heritage Centre*)

Daily check on the water ('A' Licensed inspector required)
Read previous Captain's Daily Report. Required repairs and adjustments noted. Check if completed.

- External visual check of hull (cuts, scrapes, corrosion, and 'flats' between frames. Cuts and scrapes to 30% depth acceptable. If deeper, mark plate for replacement).
- Check windows, ports, and hatches for security and watertightness.
- Check undersurface of each mainplane and tailplane.
- Check fabric of elevators and rudder for damage.
- Check floats for damage (especially around the nose).
- Check handhole covers on floats, chassis struts, and stays. Dip bilges and pump out if necessary with Enots portable bilging pump.

Interior inspection of passenger cabins:
- Inspect each cabin in turn for general cleanliness.
- Check doors and hatches for proper working and locking.
- Check windows and ports from inside, push-out windows easy to operate and clearly marked.
- Check condition of lap straps, seat upholstery, curtains, and carpets.
- Close cold air punkah louvres, set heating thermostat at 20°C, turn heating switch 'on' (if required).
- Set correct time on bulkhead clock.
- Check emergency ladders and lighting for correct operation.
- Check lavatories for cleanliness, toilet paper packs full (with a spare), lavatory floor drains clear, the shared water tank between the lavatories full (5gal).
- Check pantry water tank full (5gal), first-aid kit complete, emergency rations in place.
- Check steward's call system working, indicator lights on indicator board all 'out', and the stowage and operation of the fire extinguishers throughout the 'boat.

Interior inspection of mooring compartment:
- Check mooring hatch closed.
- Check retractable mooring bollard with mooring cable secured on the slip line, anchor stowed, eyelet on the end of the rope anchor cable ready to slip over bollard, drogues and drogue lines stowed in their containers, spare wire rope storm pennant in its stowed position, boat hook and fenders ready for use.
- Visible internal structure of the hull in the mooring compartment and aft of the passenger accommodation inspected for general condition of the frames, plating, and intercostals (any work carried out on the frames and intercostals requires a 'B' or AID Licence).

Interior inspection of freight rooms:
- Check freight nets, webbing straps, and duckboards in the flight clerk's office and aft freight room.
- Examine general condition of exposed parts of hull, frames, plating, and intercostals. Mark any damage for replacement.
- Where visible, lubricate (or grease) control cables, specially the thrust race at base of rudder.
- Control cables with not more than two broken strands passed.

Check date of last weekly bilge inspection:
- Inspection traps to the bilges opened up if required (at least once per week).
- Dip hull bilges and pump out with the Saunders bilging pump if necessary (5–10gal of water admissible).
- Greater volume of bilge water may require remedial work to the planing bottom.

Inspection of control deck:
- Check filler for the heating system (distilled water up to red line).
- Check handles of air supply valves in line with the ducts.
- Check clean removable filters in air ducts.
- If fuelling has been completed, check contents of the fuel tanks.
- Check windscreen, the direct vision panels of the coupé and the ports examined for defects, operation, and cleanliness.
- Check instruments on the dashboard for operation and security.
- Check pilots' seats and lap straps for wear.
- Remove control lock, try flight controls hard over each way.
- Replace control lock (ailerons and rudder 'neutral', elevators fully 'down').
- Check oil levels of throttle and mixture Exactor transmitter controls (sight gauges in throttle box), top up as required through plug on transmitter unit (mixture of one part DTD 44/C Flowex E or Shell No 1 anti-freezing oil to two parts of kerosene). 'Spongy' operation at the end of a stroke indicates air in the pipeline, requiring bleeding.
- Check bow and wing searchlights (turn 'on–off'). Turn bow searchlight 'out–up' and 'down–in'.
- Run flaps to 'full out' position for inspection from the mainplanes.
- Wind elevator and rudder trimming tabs in both directions and return.
- Check flags and ensigns for a full complement.

*Engine and airscrew check – carried out from the
mainplanes, via the ladder and out through the escape hatch
to the top of the hull, complete with a small tool kit. ('C'
Licence required for engine inspections):*

■ Check pitot head covers 'off', heads clean.
■ Examine mainplanes for damage, inspection covers over
the control runs in place and screwed up, navigation light
covers and attachments secure.
■ Inspect ailerons and flap guides for condition, grease flap
runners on extended flaps if required.
■ Examine metal and fabric surfaces of rudder and elevators
for excessive play and damage.
■ Note any signs of corrosion to the aileron levers, hinges,
and controls.
■ Trim tab hinges lubricated as required. The flaps
brought 'in'.
■ Open maintenance platforms on each side of each
engine (centre screw of the cover unscrewed to free it,
hand wheels inside mainplane, unscrewed and pushed
backwards to free the retaining hooks allowing the
platform to be opened forwards).
■ Open oil tank filler cap doors and oil tank circulating
chamber, and dipstick doors on nacelles. Unscrew caps.
Dip tanks.
■ Close and secure oil tank filler cap covers (hand
tight only).
■ Fit rain plugs to exhaust pipes (to be removed
before flight).
■ Remove engine cowling panels in turn.
■ Check throttle and mixture controls, operation of the air
intake shutter, and tightness of all main nuts and bolts.
■ Check that the weight-loaded slow-running cut-out
controls free (operated from the control deck).
■ Pegasus engines. Examine valve springs on each piston
to ensure that all intact. Remove spark plugs to cylinders
4, 5, 6 and 7, clean and replace.
■ Check HT leads, connections to the spark plugs secured.
New Tel-tachometer discs inserted.
■ Replace engine cowlings.
■ Check airscrew blades for scratches and dents (slight
damage removed by scraping or filing and polishing).
Check airscrews for tightness on the hub, hub tight on the
shaft and correctly locked.
■ Close maintenance platforms. Return to control deck.
■ Start engines in turn (cowling gills wound 'open',
airscrews in 'fine' pitch, mixture at 'normal').

■ When oil temperature is 15°C, open throttles up to 'full'
(10sec max.). Check boost by moving mixture levers to
'rich', noting flame, and back to 'normal'. The flames
were:

Very rich	Smoky and long irregular blue flames
Rich	Long narrow blue flames
Normal	Short bluish Bunsen-type flame
Weak	Normal blue flame changing to narrow transparent dull green
Very weak	Almost transparent flame with red centre, possible popping back to carburettor.

■ Throttle back to 1,500rpm.
■ Check magnetos, turn 'on–off–on', change airscrew
pitch, 'fine' to 'coarse' to 'fine'. Listen for out-of-balance
airscrews producing a characteristic rhythmic beat.
■ Check engine acceleration for flat spots and for rough
running, throttle back to 500rpm to check slow running.
■ While engines are running, carry out autopilot maker's
instructions for pre-flight checks.
■ Shut down engines, throttle back, turn magnetos 'off', pull
cut-off levers 'off', and close cowling gills.

If required for a service, Kilfrost anti-icing paste was applied
by brush or palette knife to leading edges of mainplanes,
aerial mast (avoiding insulators), tailplanes, and fin. It was
also smeared on the joints of the servo and trim tabs on
rudder and trim tabs on elevators, noses of floats, and
leading edges of float chassis struts.

The Daily Certificate for flight was then signed.

ABOVE Engine maintenance at Durban. *(British Airways Speedbird Heritage Centre)*

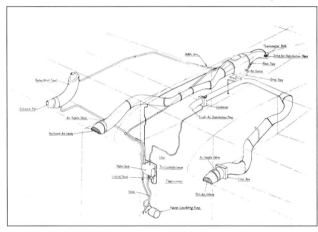

ABOVE Heating and ventilation system, passenger aircraft.
(Author's collection)

10-hour engine check ('C' Licence required for engine inspections):

■ Check valve clearances. Reset if required.

■ Remove engine sump filters. Clean and replace.

■ Check magnetos. Clean contact breakers.

■ Airscrews in 'coarse' pitch. Lubricate airscrew hub nipples with Mobile No 2 oil. Grease exposed cylinder.

■ Remove counterweight bearing caps. Grease bearings.

■ Check hubs for leaks.

20-hour engine and airframe check

■ Beach aircraft and haul out. (Max. allowable weight on beaching chassis 39,000lb)

■ Hose down underwater surfaces to remove salt deposits.

■ All engines. Carry out 10-hour engine check.

■ Each engine. Remove spark plugs, clean and replace. Check compression.

■ Check engine cylinder rockers, brackets, and upper end of pushrods. Lubricate rocker-adjusting screw.

■ Flush out fuel system. Replace pipes. Adjust tank controls.

40-hour engine and airframe check

■ Carry out 20-hour engine and airframe check.

■ Each engine. Drain and clean carburettor float chambers.

■ Drain down and flush oil coolers.

■ Lubricate magnetos.

■ Clean distributors.

■ Lubricate engine valve spring felt pads (DTD 109 oil).

■ Lubricate fuel pump bearings.

■ Check and recalibrate engine boost gauges.

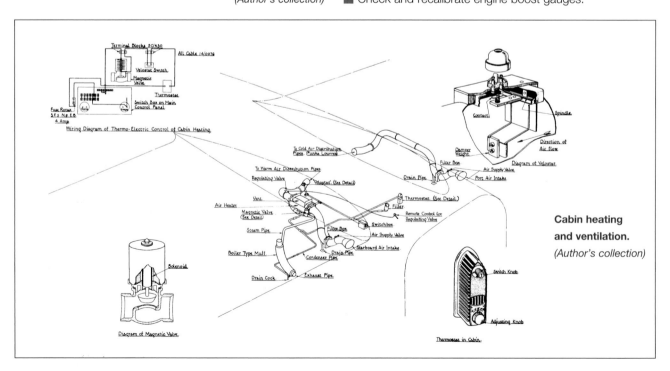

Cabin heating and ventilation.
(Author's collection)

ABOVE AND RIGHT *Castor* undergoes maintenance inside a hangar. *(British Airways Speedbird Heritage Centre)*

- Drain down and flush out engine oil system. (Check oil filters for metal particles).
- Examine, clean, and lubricate control wires, chains, levers, bearings, and pulleys in the mainplanes and hull.
- Remove inspection patches on rudder and elevators for internal inspection.
- Inspect ailerons and flaps. Check ball-races in flap guides.
- Remove float inspection covers. Examine interior. Clean and recoat with lanolin.
- Check float attachments and bracing wires, top and bottom.
- Carry out maker's instructions for electrical system, generators, bow and wing (starboard) searchlights.
- Examine heating and ventilating systems throughout (special attention to bonding).
- Take up carpets and flooring on the lower deck. Remove for examination. Open up bilges, pump out as required. Clean and recoat with lanolin.

120-hour engine and airframe check
- Check airframe for alignment. Plus/minus ¾in allowed on diagonals.
- Open up patches on the mainplanes, elevators, and rudder for examination of all control runs for wear and corrosion.
- Check solid mahogany servo and trim tabs for oil and water soakage. Check for twist – ¼in allowable.
- Check fuel and oil pipe lines for chafing and corrosion.
- Grease engine cylinder head rockers and felt pads.
- Replace Tecalemit oil filter elements.
- Examine inside of mainplane for fuel leaks and water penetration from the tank cover.
- Recoat underwater surfaces of the hull and floats with lanolin as required.

210-hour engine and airframe check
- Carry out 120-hour engine and airframe check, including detailed inspection of the hull interior and floats.

- Change spark plugs.
- Drain oil system. Inspect oil tanks.
- Check operation flying and engine controls.

250-hour engine check
- Remove engines in rotation for complete overhaul. Send to Croydon (UK 'boats), Durban (Horseshoe Route 'boats), Sydney (QANTAS 'boats), or Auckland (TEAL 'boats).

270-hour airscrew check
- Remove airscrews in rotation for complete overhaul.
- After stripping, examine blades under magnification for scratches, dismantle the hubs (subject steel parts to crack detection), reassemble dry, balance, and check the blades for angle.
- After balancing, strip down airscrews, grease, and reassemble.

312-hour engine and airframe check
- General hull inspection, cleaning, full and detailed check of the whole of the airframe, engines, and electrical equipment.
- After inspection, carry out engine runs.
- Launch aircraft. Remove beaching gear.
- Swing compass.
- Ballast to take-off weight.
- Moor up ready for test flight.

RIGHT Empire 'boat airscrew. *(British Airways Speedbird Heritage Centre)*

FAR RIGHT A part-sectional illustration of a de Havilland controllable-pitch airscrew in low pitch.

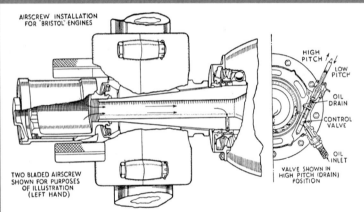

AIRSCREW INSTALLATION FOR 'BRISTOL' ENGINES

HIGH PITCH
LOW PITCH
OIL DRAIN
CONTROL VALVE
OIL INLET

TWO BLADED AIRSCREW SHOWN FOR PURPOSES OF ILLUSTRATION (LEFT HAND)

VALVE SHOWN IN HIGH PITCH (DRAIN) POSITION

ABOVE The de Havilland controllable-pitch airscrew for Bristol engines. A two-bladed airscrew is shown for the purposes of illustration.

RIGHT Engine and airscrew slinging. *(Shorts)*

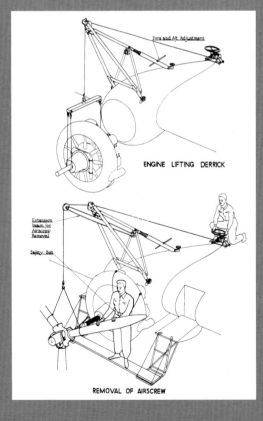

Fore and Aft Adjustment

ENGINE LIFTING DERRICK

Extension beam for Airscrew Removal

Safety Belt

REMOVAL OF AIRSCREW

AIRSCREW OVERHAUL

The routine maintenance of the airscrew varied to some extent with the type of installation and conditions under which it was operated, but in every case a schedule had to be adopted to ensure the airscrew received regular attention. Central to this procedure were the following checks:

- The airscrew remains tight on the airscrew shaft.
- The piston leathers are securely held.
- It is adequately lubricated.
- The fastenings and locking arrangements remain unimpaired.
- The rate of wear and tear of moving parts is proceeding normally.
- There is no damage to the blades, eg cracks and abrasions (particularly in the case of the Empire 'boats, corrosion by seawater)
- To remove (or dismount) the airscrew it is first necessary to remove the cylinder cover and withdraw the split pins securing the piston locking ring to the lip of the spider; when unscrewing, the piston will withdraw the airscrew from the taper.
- A sling is then made fast around two of the airscrew blade roots and the weight is taken by means of tackle, when the airscrew can be drawn off the shaft and lowered.
- To reinstall the airscrew these operations are reversed with the addition that before mounting the airscrew, the splines of the engine shaft should be smeared with anti-seizing compound recommended by the engine maker, in this case Bristol's.

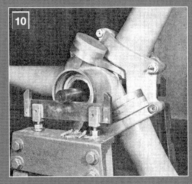
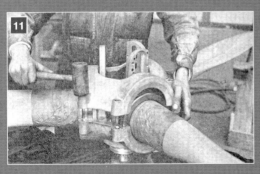

1 Removing the counterweight bearing shafts.

2 Unscrewing the piston from the assembly sleeve with the aid of a piston wrench and tommy bar.

3 Removing the cylinder, piston, piston locking ring, snap ring and front cone from the airscrew.

4 After removing the barrel bolts, separate the halves of the barrel by using a lever in the slots provided in the joint face on the rear half, lifting the top half of the barrel ...

5 ... and lowering the bottom half.

6 Removing the thrust-bearing cages.

7 Withdrawing the blade from the spider.

8 Checking blade angles.

9 Lowering the airscrew on the balancing ways. A balancing mandrel (a replica of the engine shaft used when stripping and reassembling the airscrew) is supported at each end by so-called knife edges mounted on sturdy metal frame towers.

10 A close-up of a 5000-size three-blade airscrew on the knife edges, showing the application of lead wool in the hollow barrel bolts (see the bolt at top right). These bores are finally closed with sealing caps. Balancing is carried out in a draught-proof cubicle.

11 Reassembling the top half barrel.

12 An engine test is carried out to check correct operation of the overhauled propeller. This is at Hythe, Southampton, in 1939. *(British Airways Speedbird Heritage Centre)*

Appendix

'C' class Empire flying boat names

The names of the 42 Empire 'boats were chosen from a full list of 125, a diverse mixture of the classical, the literary, the national, the regional, persons, or just names beginning with the initial letter 'C'. All the 'boats were first entered on the UK registry. The Qantas Empire Airways (QEA) and Tasman Empire Airways Limited (TEAL) 'boats were re-registered when taken on their national registers.

(Certificate of Airworthiness – CoA.)

The names given to the IAL, BOAC, QEA and TEAL 'boats were:

S795 S.23 G-ADHL *Canopus*. Ordered 24 January 1935; Registered 17 June 1935; CoA 20 October 1936; Delivered 22 October 1936; Broken up at Hythe 23 October 1946.

S804 S.23 G-ADHM *Caledonia*. Ordered 27 May 1935; Registered 17 June 1935; CoA December 1936; Delivered 4 December 1936; Broken up at Hythe 23 March 1947.

S811 S.23 G-ADUT *Centaurus*. Ordered 24 January 1935; Registered 7 October 1935; CoA 28 October 1936; Delivered 7 December 1936; Transferred to QEA September 1939; Impressed into RAAF as A18-10; Destroyed (enemy action) at moorings, Broome, WA 3 March 1942.

S812 S.23 G-ADUU *Cavalier*. Ordered 27 May 1935; Registered 7 October 1935; CoA 26 November 1936; Delivered 10 December 1936; Crashed in North Atlantic 21 January 1939.

S813 S.23 G-ADUV *Cambria*. Ordered

BELOW **G-ADVE**, *Centurion*, **crashed near Calcutta in June 1939.** *(British Airways Speedbird Heritage Centre)*

27 May 1935; Registered 7 October 1935; CoA 15 January 1937; Delivered 21 January 1937; Broken up at Hythe January 1947.

S814 S.23 G-ADUW *Castor*. Ordered 27 May 1935; Registered 7 October 1935; CoA 23 December 1936; Delivered 2 January 1937; Broken up at Hythe 4 February 1947.

S815 S.23 G-ADUX *Cassiopeia*. Ordered 27 May 1935; Registered 7 October 1935; CoA 25 January 1937; Delivered 1 February 1937; Crashed Sabang 29 December 1941.

S816 S.23 G-ADUY *Capella*. Ordered 27 May 1935; Registered 7 October 1935; CoA 16 February 1937; Delivered 16 February 1937; Holed in Batavia Harbour 12 March 1939.

S817 S.23 G-ADUZ *Cygnus*. Ordered 27 May 1935; Registered 7 October 1935; CoA 1 March 1937; Delivered 3 March 1937. Crashed on take-off at Brindisi 5 December 1937.

S818 S.23 G-ADVA *Capricornus*. Ordered 27 May 1935; Registered 7 October 1935; CoA 14 March 1937; Delivered 16 March 1937; Crashed Ouroux in France 24 March 1937.

S819 S.23 G-ADVB *Corsair*. Ordered 27 May 1935; Registered 7 October 1935; CoA 3 April 1937; Delivered 8 April 1937; Broken up at Hythe 20 January 1947.

S820 S.23 G-ADVC *Courtier*. Ordered 27 May 1935; Registered 7 October 1935; CoA 21 April 1937; Delivered 24 April 1937. Crashed at Athens 1 October 1937.

S821 S.23 G-ADVD *Challenger*. Ordered 27 May 1935; Registered 7 October 1935; CoA 8 May 1937; Delivered 6 May 1937; Crashed in Mozambique 1 May 1939.

S822 S.23 G-ADVE *Centurion*. Ordered 27 May 1935; Registered 7 October 1935; CoA 29 May 1937; Delivered 29 May 1937; Crashed at Calcutta 12 June 1939.

S838 S.23 G-AETV *Coriolanus*. VH-ABG. Ordered 2 September 1935; Registered 1 March 1937; CoA 17 June 1937; Delivered 17 June 1937; Broken up at Sydney end of 1947.

S839 S.23 G-AETW *Calpurnia*. Ordered 2 September 1935; Registered 1 March 1937; CoA 28 June 1937; Delivered 30 June 1937; Crashed at Lake Habbaniyah 27 November 1938.

S840 S.23 G-AETX *Ceres*. Ordered 2 September 1935; Registered 1 March 1937; CoA 16 July 1937; Delivered 17 July 1937; Destroyed by fire at Durban 1 December 1942.

S841 S.23 G-AETY *Clio* AX 659. Ordered 2 September 1935; Registered 1 March 1937; CoA 26 July 1937; Delivered 30 July 1937; Crashed at Loch Indal 22 August 1941.

S842 S.23 G-AETZ *Circe*. Ordered 2 September 1935; Registered 1 March 1937; CoA 16 August 1937; Delivered 16 August 1937; Lost without trace between Broome and Tijlatjap 28 February 1942.

S843 S.23 G-AEUA *Calypso* A18-11. Ordered 2 September 1935; Registered 1 March 1937; CoA 26 August 1937; Delivered 27 August 1937; Transferred to QEA September 1939; Impressed into RAAF; Crashed in sea off Daru, Papua New Guinea, damaged and sank 8 August 1942.

S844 S.23 G-AEUB *Camilla* VH-ADU. Ordered 2 September 1935; Registered 1 March 1937; CoA 13 September 1937; Delivered 13 September 1937; To QANTAS August 1942; Crashed at Port Moresby 22 April 1943.

S845 S.23 G-AEUC *Corinna*. Ordered 2 September 1935; Registered 1 March 1937; CoA 25 September 1937; Delivered 29 September 1937; Destroyed (enemy action) at moorings, Broome, WA 3 March 1942.

S846 S.23 G-AEUD *Cordelia* AX 660. Ordered 2 September 1935; Registered 1 March 1937; CoA 9 October 1937; Delivered 9 October 1937; Broken up at Hythe early April 1947.

S847 S.23 G-AEUE *Cameronian*. Ordered
2 September 1935; Registered 1 March 1937;
CoA 23 October 1937; Delivered 23 October
1937; Broken up at Hythe January 1947.

S848 S.23 G-AEUF *Corinthian*. Ordered
2 September 1935; Registered 1 March 1937;
CoA 9 November 1937; Delivered 6 November
1937; Crashed at Darwin 22 March 1942.

S849 S.23 G-AEUG *Coogee* (originally
named *Cheviot*). Ordered 2 September 1935;
Registered 1 March 1937; CoA 8 January
1938; Delivered 3 January 1938. Transferred
to QEA September 1939; Impressed into RAAF
as VH-ABC A18-12; Crashed at Townsville,
Queensland 1 March 1942.

S850 S.23 G-AEUH *Corio* VH-ABD (originally
named *Coolin*). Ordered 2 September 1935;
Registered 1 March 1937; CoA 10 February
1938; Delivered 10 February 1938; To QEA
October 1938. Shot down near Koepang
30 January 1942.

S851 S.23 G-AEUI *Coorong* VH-ABE (originally
named *Calpe*). Ordered 2 September 1935;
Registered 1 March 1937; CoA 26 February
1938; Delivered 26 February1938; To QEA
September 1938; Broken up at Hythe
10 February 1947.

S876 S.23-G-AFBJ *Carpentaria* VH-ABA. Ordered
27 April 1937; Registered 26 August 1937; CoA
November 1937; Delivered 3 December 1937; To
QEA June 1938; Broken up at Hythe 19 January
1947.

S877 S.23 G-AFBK *Coolangatta* VH-ABB,
A18-13. Ordered 22 June 1937; Registered
26 August 1937; CoA 19 April 1938; Delivered
18 December 1937; To QEA 18 March 1938;
Impressed into RAAF 8 November 1941;
Returned to QEA 29 July 1943; Crashed at Rose
Bay, Sydney, NSW 11 October 1944.

S878 S.23 G-AFBL *Cooee* VH-ABF. Ordered
22 June 1937; Registered 26 August 1937;
CoA 30 March 1938; Delivered 30 March 1938;
Broken up at Hythe 2 February 1947.

S879 S.30 G-AFCT *Champion*. Ordered
21 October 1937; Registered 15 November
1937; CoA 27 October 1938; Delivered
28 October 1938; Broken up at Hythe
16 March 1947.

S880 S.30 G-AFCU *Cabot* V3137. Ordered
21 October 1937; Registered 15 November
1937; CoA 8 March 1939; Delivered March 1939;
Destroyed near Bodø, Norway 5/6 May 1940.

S881 S.30 G-AFCV *Caribou* V3138. Ordered 21

October 1937; Registered 15 November 1937; CoA July 1939; Delivered 7 or 13 July 1939; Destroyed Bodø, Norway 5 May 1940.

S882 S.30 G-AFCW *Connemara*. Ordered 21 October 1937; Registered 15 November 1937; CoA 25 March 1939; Delivered 25 March 1939; Destroyed by fire at Southampton Water 19 June 1939.

S883 S.30 G-AFCX *Clyde*. Ordered 21 October 1937; Registered 15 November 1937; CoA 29 March 1939; Delivered 30 March 1939; Wrecked at Lisbon 14 February 1941.

S884 S.30 G-AFCY. Originally launched as ZK-AMA *Aotearoa*; Re-registered ZK-AMC and renamed *Awarua*. Ordered 21 October 1937; Registered 15 November 1937; CoA April 1939; Delivered 21 April 1939; Broken up at Auckland August 1948.

S885 S.30 G-AFCZ *Australia* (originally named *Canterbury* and later renamed *Clare*). Ordered 21 October 1937; Registered 15 November 1937; CoA 6 April 1939; Delivered 24 April 1939; Destroyed by fire off Bathurst, West Africa 14/15 September 1942.

S886 S.30 G-AFDA. Originally launched as ZK-AMC *Awarua*; Re-registered ZK-AMA and renamed *Aotearoa*. Ordered 21 October 1937; Registered 15 November 1937; CoA May 1939; Delivered 25 May 1939; Broken up at Auckland after October 1947.

S1003 S.30 G-AFKZ *Cathay*. Date of order not known; Registered 10 November 1938; CoA 26 February 1940; Delivered 8 March 1940; Broken up at Hythe 9 March 1947.

S1025 S.33 G-AFPZ *Clifton* VH-ACD A18-14. Ordered 7 June 1939; Registered 27 January 1939; CoA 7 June 1939; Delivered 17 March 1940; Leased to RAAF 12 March 1942; Released from RAAF 26 June 1943 and bought by QEA; Crashed at Rose Bay, Sydney, NSW during a training accident 18 November 1944.

S1026 S.33 G-AFRA *Cleopatra*. Ordered 7 June 1939; Registered 27 January 1939; CoA 8 May 1940; Delivered 10 May 1940; Broken up at Hythe 4 November 1946.

S1027 S.33 G-AFRB Not named. Ordered 7 June 1939; Registered 27 January 1939; Hull stored 12 April 1940; Scrapped 1943.

BELOW G-AFBK, *Coolangatta,* **was transferred to Queensland Empire Airways as VH-ABB before being impressed into the RAAF as A18-13.** *(British Airways Speedbird Heritage Centre)*

Index